Daniel March

Walks and homes of Jesus

Daniel March

Walks and homes of Jesus

ISBN/EAN: 9783744648356

Printed in Europe, USA, Canada, Australia, Japan

Cover: Foto ©Lupo / pixelio.de

More available books at **www.hansebooks.com**

WALKS AND HOMES

OF

JESUS.

BY THE
Rev. DANIEL MARCH, D.D.,
AUTHOR OF "NIGHT SCENES IN THE BIBLE."

ELEVENTH THOUSAND.

ZIEGLER & McCURDY:
PHILADELPHIA, PA.; CINCINNATI, O.; ST. LOUIS, MO.;
SPRINGFIELD, MASS.

Entered according to the Act of Congress, in the year 1866, by
WM. L. HILDEBURN, TREASURER,
in trust for the
PRESBYTERIAN PUBLICATION COMMITTEE.
In the Clerk's Office of the District Court for the Eastern District of Pennsylvania.

WESTCOTT & THOMSON,
Stereotypers.

JAS. B. RODGERS,
PRINTER.

PREFACE.

N the composition of the following pages an attempt has been made to look upon our Lord as he was seen by the men of his time, and to combine with that view the more mature and instructed impressions which spring from faith in his redeeming work and his divine nature. Taking the Gospel record for our guide, and keeping the present aspect of Palestine ever in mind, we have sought an introduction to the HOMES where he dwelt; we have ventured to join him in his earthly WALKS. The natural features of the country and the known customs of the time have been wrought into the sketches with some degree of freedom, in order to set forth the human and historic reality of the divine Personage, whose abode with men is the greatest event in all the past, and whose death on the cross for the world's salvation, will continue to be the wonder of ages and of eternity.

The towns and cities, in which our Lord made his abode, have indeed greatly changed with the lapse of time, and some of them can scarcely be identified. But still, the natural features of the country confirm the inspired record beyond all question, and the sacred localities, so far as recognised, help us greatly in giving form and reality to our faith in the great fact of the divine incarnation. We find it easier to believe that the Son of God was seen on earth in fashion as a man, when we gaze on the field where angels announced his birth; when we visit the secluded vale where he was hidden from the world for thirty years; when we climb the mount where he was seen in his glory; when we walk upon the silent shore of the sea of Galilee; when we descend the slope of Olivet and cross the Kidron, or muse beneath the olive trees of Gethsemane. These "holy places," however changed by time, or desecrated by superstition, still help us to see Jesus as he was in the world, and so more fully to believe in the truths which he taught and the work which he accomplished.

It has not been thought necessary or appropriate, in a purely practical work, to assign reasons or authorities for a few assumptions that have been made, such as that Tabor is the mount of the Transfiguration, Tell Hûm the site of Capernaum, the Horns of Hattin the scene of the Sermon on the Mount.

The writer has found the task of visiting the Homes and tracing the Walks of Jesus with men, its own reward. He would fain hope, that what has been written, may awaken in some reader's heart, a desire for a closer Walk with Jesus on earth, and for a blessed Home with him forever in heaven.

CONTENTS.

I.
BETHLEHEM.. 9

II.
NAZARETH... 45

III.
CAPERNAUM.. 67

IV.
BETHESDA.. 123

V.
TABOR... 145

VI.
JERICHO... 175

VII.
BETHANY... 197

VIII.
JERUSALEM... 293

ILLUSTRATIONS.

			PAGE
1	THE FRIENDS OF JESUS. FRONTISPIECE. STEEL-PLATE-ENGRAVING.		
2	MODERN BETHLEHEM...		13
3.	WILDERNESS OF JUDEA. VIEW FROM THE MOUTH OF THE CAVE OF ADULLAM, LOOKING EASTWARD TO THE MOUNTAINS OF MOAB BEYOND THE DEAD SEA...	*F. Graham, Photo.*	16
4.	BETHLEHEM, WITH ROAD TO JERUSALEM IN FOREGROUND...	*F. Graham, Photo.*	24
5.	THE BIRTH OF CHRIST...	*W. L. Sheppard.*	37
6.	THE FLIGHT INTO EGYPT...	*W. L. Sheppard.*	42
7.	MODERN NAZARETH...		48
8.	VIEW FROM ABOVE NAZARETH, LOOKING SOUTHWARD...	*Rev. S. C. Malan.*	54
9.	THE SEA OF TIBERIAS...	*Rev. S. C. Malan.*	67
10.	FISHERMEN OF THE SEA OF GALILEE...	*Rev. S. C. Malan.*	75
11.	PARALYTIC LET DOWN THROUGH THE ROOF FOR HEALING...	*Rev. S. C. Malan.*	96
12.	CHRIST FEEDING THE FIVE THOUSAND...	*W. L. Sheppard.*	100
13.	DISTANT VIEW OF THE LAKE OF GALILEE...		107
14.	FISHERMAN OF THE SEA OF GALILEE CASTING HIS NET...	*Rev. S. C. Malan.*	120
15.	THE HEALING AT THE POOL OF BETHESDA...	*W. L. Sheppard.*	129
16.	MOUNT TABOR, SOUTH FACE...		149
17.	ANCIENT CASTLE ON THE ROAD FROM JERICHO TO JERUSALEM.	*Rev. H. S. Osborn.*	175
18.	SITE OF JERICHO, WITH THE ONLY REMAINING STONE BUILDING ON THE RIGHT...	*F. Graham, Photo.*	190
19.	HEALING THE BLIND MAN AT JERICHO...	*W. L. Sheppard.*	194
20.	MODERN BETHANY...		197
21.	PASS IN THE ROAD FROM JERUSALEM TO JERICHO...	*Rev. S. C. Malan.*	204
22.	THE JORDAN NEAR JERICHO...	*F. Graham, Photo.*	236
23.	BETHANY, FROM THE ROAD TO JERICHO, AND LOOKING TOWARD THE MOUNT OF OLIVES ON THE RIGHT...	*F. Graham, Photo.*	268
24.	THE ENTRY TO JERUSALEM...	*W. L. Sheppard.*	296
25.	VALLEY OF KEDRON AND MOUNT OF OLIVES...		299
26.	PATHWAY FROM BETHANY TO JERUSALEM, WITH THE GARDEN OF GETHSEMANE AND NORTH-EAST CORNER OF THE WALL OF JERUSALEM...	*F. Graham, Photo.*	306
27.	OLIVE TREES IN GETHSEMANE...	*F. Graham, Photo.*	309

BETHLEHEM.

Let us now go even unto Bethlehem, and see this thing which is come to pass, which the Lord hath made known unto us.—
LUKE ii. 15.

WALKS AND HOMES OF JESUS.

I.

BETHLEHEM.

HE one name, which makes Palestine "The Holy Land" for all the world and for all time, is JESUS.

The three places of surpassing interest in the earthly life of Jesus, are Bethlehem, Nazareth, Jerusalem. In all our studies of his divine work and character, we feel ourselves drawn with peculiar attraction to the manger where he was born, to the home where he lived, to the cross where he died. Over Bethlehem, the star of hope dawned upon a darkened and despairing world. At Nazareth, the divine Life dwelt in the habitations of men. On Calvary, the conflict with death was complete, and the cross of shame was changed to the sceptre of power and the throne of glory. The benignant heavens shed sweet influences, and the angel host sung for joy, over the divine birth at Bethlehem. The wondering heavens looked down in silence, and the waiting angels hushed their songs, while the divine Life walked unrecognized, side by side with peasants and carpenters, for thirty years among the hills of Nazareth. The witnessing heavens put on sackcloth of astonishment, and the convulsed earth was rent in agony, when the divine Sufferer of Calvary cried, in darkness and desolation of soul, as if God had forsaken him.

To Bethlehem, the first of these three "holy places" in Palestine, our attention is drawn by the opening scene in the Saviour's earthly life. We may well desire to learn all we can of the sacred spot which God had chosen to signalize through all coming ages, by the incarnation of his divine and eternal Son. We make pilgrimages to the birth-place of patriots and heroes. We build monuments to the mighty dead. We trace out the source and the march of great revolutions. We gaze with inspired enthusiasm upon the field where nations met in the shock of arms. With a more profound and reverent interest may we study the place, the time and the circumstances of the greatest event in the world's history, the coming of the Son of God to accomplish the world's redemption.

It is by the awful and infinite mystery of the divine incarnation, that the deep chasm between heaven and earth is bridged over, and a way cast up, for angels to pass to and fro, on messages of love. It is by the incarnation, that the Holy One dwells in the habitations of men, and children of wrath are made sons and daughters of the Lord Almighty. When we consider the frailty of this mortal state, the infirmity that burdens our loftiest effort, the dimness that clouds our clearest vision, the sinfulness that paralyzes our noblest purposes, the depravity that poisons the life blood of our hearts, it seems almost too much for belief, that the everlasting God should take upon himself our flesh, and should bear the weight of our infirmities, in sorrow and suffering, to the cross. But upon this one truth hangs the redemption of a lost world. There is no revelation of the divine mercy too great for us to receive, when once we recognize in the babe of Bethlehem, the mighty One, whose goings forth have been from of old, even from everlasting.

Guided by such information as we can gather from all sources, "let us now go even unto Bethlehem," and see the place where the King of glory appeared in the form of a servant, and clothed in the garb of our frail mortality, eighteen hundred years ago.

The town of Bethlehem is six miles to the south of Jerusalem, a little to the east of the main road to Hebron. The Syrian Mountains, extending northward to Hermon and Lebanon, and southward to the Arabian desert, lie upon the whole face of Palestine, like some vast centipede, with rocky arms of limestone hills extending east and west, between narrow valleys and winding glens running down to the Jordan and the Dead Sea on the one side, and to the plains of Sharon and Carmel on the other. On one of these ridges, extending only a mile from the central chain, stands Bethlehem. It is closed around on every side, save one, by higher hills. To the south-east is Beth-haccerem, on which the sign of fire was lifted up

Modern Bethlehem.

Walks and Homes of Jesus.

for the gathering of the tribes, when the trumpet of war was blown in Tekoa. South-east is Gibeah of Judah, from whose rocky heights the wild mountaineers looked down upon the field of Ephesdammim, when Israel and the Philistines put the battle in array, army against army, and the shepherd boy of Bethlehem, slew the giant warrior of Gath. North-east, cutting off the view of Jerusalem and the Mount of Olives, is the rocky crest and castellated convent of Mar Elias, from whose time-worn towers the traveller looks down into the gorge of the Jordan, and along the melancholy shores of the Dead Sea.

Entering the gate of Bethlehem at the west, we climb the same ascent up which Joseph and Mary toiled, weary and belated, on that memorable night, which has been made an era for all subsequent ages, and the source of new hopes and a new history, for all mankind. Eighteen centuries have wrought but little change upon the stone-built town and the strife-loving people. The arched gateway of the wall; the narrow, uneven, broken foot-path of the main street, difficult to travel by day and dangerous by night; the white tomb-like stone houses, presenting a windowless wall to the street, scattered irregularly for a mile's length along the ridge of the hill, and sometimes so near each other as to touch and cover the traveller with their projecting balconies; the still narrower lanes and alleys, running off right and left, and opening a pathway to still gloomier stone huts, and stables, and caves in the rock, all equally the homes of man and beast;—these are to-day, substantially the same that they were, on that night, when the weary strangers from Nazareth groped their way through the whole length of the dark, crooked and stony street, to the khan at the eastern extremity there at last to find lodgings with the beasts of the stall.

Standing upon the walls of Bethlehem, or upon the domed roof of one of its limestone houses, we see the same landscape that was seen by Mary and Joseph, David and Samuel, Ruth and Naomi, Rachel and Jacob. On the north, east and south, the cultivated slopes of the hill descend to the plain in terraces, with as much regularity as the galleries of an amphitheatre. In the early spring, vines hang in gay festoons from bank to bank. The wide, branching fig fences the garden plots with its living wall of dark green foliage. The silvery leaves of the olive glisten in cascades of evergreen, from terrace to terrace. The grapes of Bethlehem are noted for their strong, aromatic flavor, and the whole air is perfumed with the smell of the vintage. The figs that ripen on the Southern slopes of the hill are remembered by travellers as they remember the wells of the desert and the waters of the Nile. In the valley below the town, and on the narrow plain beyond, there are fields of wheat and barley, where, in the month of April, the reapers may be seen, followed by the gleaners, just as Ruth gleaned after the young men of Boaz in the same field, thirty-one hundred and seventy-five years ago.

The green terraces and the little narrow valleys of cultivated ground around Bethlehem, are made more refreshing to the eye by contrast with the wilderness of Judah in full sight beyond. The view in that direction is bounded by hills of white limestone, thrown confusedly together, like waves when the winds suddenly change and seas cross each other in wild discord. The hills are cloven by narrow waterless ravines, and the mouths of many caverns open upon their steep sides, and farther away the glens contract into wild, deep gorges, or slope off with a rapid descent to the dismal shores of the Dead Sea. Not a solitary tree, nor a spot of green earth can be seen along the whole outline of scorched and blasted hills and robber-haunted glens which bound the view toward the wilderness of Judah and the mountains of Moab. Standing upon the ridge of Bethlehem and looking in that direction, one seems to have landed upon an island of green in an ocean of desolation.

The birth of Jesus is the great event which gives sacredness and importance to this little town, perched upon a hill-top and pushed aside from the march of armies and the merchandise of nations. And yet Bethlehem itself had a history before the world's Redeemer took refuge in its humble stall. Before the Hebrews were a people, before Jerusalem had its name, Jacob came back from his long exile in Padan-

The Wilderness of Judea from the mouth of the Cave of Adullam, looking eastward, to the mountains of Moab beyond the Dead Sea.

Walks and Homes of Jesus.

aram, journeying toward Hebron. The train of his servants and camels and sheep and goats was a great host; and they came leisurely along the rough and winding road from the north, filling the whole valley with their multitude.

When within a mile of Bethlehem, just as the camels came down from the steep, stony track of the road into the green valley, Rachel, the younger and the most beloved of the Patriarch's wives, fainted with the pangs of travail, and as she lay in agony by the roadside, and her soul was departing, she named her new-born child, Benoni, "son of my sorrow." More than forty years afterward, when Jacob himself was old and blind and dying, he commemorated in his last words the place and the bitter agony which took from him his beloved Rachel and gave him Benjamin by the road-side in sight of the hill of Bethlehem.

And the birth of that "son of sorrow" was undoubtedly appointed at that place in the midst of a household journey, and it was recorded by the pen of inspiration to point forward seventeen hundred years, down the line of history, to a greater and more mysterious agony, when the Son of God should become a "man of sorrows," and take on himself the sins and afflictions of a lost world.

Some four hundred years after the death of Rachel, in the month of April, in the time of the barley harvest, two lonely women, mother and daughter, appeared, hungry and homeless and afflicted, in the narrow street of Bethlehem. They had come all the way from beyond the Dead Sea, across the mouth of the Jordan, up through the lonely paths of the wilderness, and the wild glens among the mountains of Judah. Their friendless condition excited the commiseration of the whole town. But the mother was proud and unhappy, and she resented all offers of sympathy or help. When the curious villagers asked in kindness who she was, she said they might call her anything that meant wretchedness and misery; for "the Almighty had dealt very bitterly with her."

But the daughter was gentle and affectionate, and ready to do anything to save herself and her proud-spirited old mother from starving. She even begged to be permitted to go down into the barley-field below the town, and glean after the reapers. It is hard for the stoutest heart to hold out against hunger; and so the unhappy mother let the daughter go, staying behind herself, to brood over her pride and misery in some wretched stone cabin of the town. The daughter went with more willingness to her humble toil, stooping through the hot stubble all day, gathering the bearded heads of barley with her bare hand, at night sitting down by the road-side to beat out the kernels with a stick, and carrying home a few handfuls of dry grain to pound with a stone and bake in the ashes, and so keep herself and her poor old mother alive.

And it was because that affectionate daughter performed such menial work with the grace of cheerfulness and simplicity, that she drew the attention of the lord of the field. And hence the name of Ruth stands in sacred history, as the mother of a line of kings, and the Son of God, himself was descended in his humanity from a homeless exile, who saved herself and her mother from starving, by gleaning barley all day in the hot field beneath the hill of Bethlehem.

Four generations after Ruth, there was a day when an old man with a white beard and a mournful look, came up the hill leaning on his prophet's staff, and entered the western gate of Bethlehem. When the elders of the town saw him, they trembled at his presence, for they knew that the word of the Lord came by his mouth, and wherever he appeared men were afraid that he had come to call their sins to remembrance. But he soon quieted the fears of the elders of Bethlehem by assuring them that at this time his errand was peace.

There was an old man in the village who had eight sons, seven of them full grown, giants in strength and in stature, mighty men of valor. Between them and their younger brother, there was an interval of many years. He was a boy, more youthful in appearance than in age; of fair complexion and beautiful features and goodly to look upon. The rude and stalwart brothers despised the boy for his youth and his beauty, and they treated him as if he were a slave or a girl. They set him to watch sheep and to follow the goats, as they climbed the ridges and wandered through the narrow valleys to the east of the town.

But the beautiful and fair-haired boy made good use of his shepherd life, in learning lessons suited to the people and the time. He became familiar with all the glens and ridges and high places of the wild country, from Bethlehem eastward down to the cave of Adullam and the passes of Engedi. He learned to bear hunger and heat and cold and fatigue, day and night, until he became indifferent to all extremes of temperature and all forms of danger. He could scale heights where the eagle must be bold to build her nest, and he could walk on the edge of the cliff, where the wild goats feared to climb. He could make his meal of parched corn, and drink of the mountain spring, and sleep at night with the heavens for a covering and the rock for a bed. He would attack the lion and the bear single-handed, and deliver the lambs of his flock from the fiercest of the beasts of prey. The roving Arab could not surprise him in the field or the fold, and the daring robber from the desert, learned to avoid an encounter with such a keeper.

He became familiar with mountains and winds and clouds; with pathless solitudes, and sounding storms, and starry nights. He taught his fingers to play upon the harp, and he made the waste places of the wilderness vocal with psalms of praise. He wove the glories of the sunset, and the fires of the firmament, and the shadows of the forest, and the lightnings of the tempest, and the voices of the deep, into songs that shall be sung through all coming time.

And now when Samuel the prophet called Jesse's sons to pass before him, that he might anoint the noblest, king over Israel, the seven stalwart men were rejected, and this forgotten boy was sent for to come in from the sheep-walks in the wilderness, and on him the consecrating oil was poured, in the name of the Lord, in the midst of his brethren. And so when the divine Son of David was born in Bethlehem, a thousand years afterward, he came, in the line of descent, from one who kept sheep on the neighboring hills, and wandered a fugitive and an outlaw, among the caves and glens of the wilderness beyond.

When David, in his old age, was driven from his throne and from Jerusalem, by the unnatural rebellion of his son Absalom, he took refuge among the mountains of Gilead, to the east of the Jordan. An old chief among the mountain tribes, Barzillai by name, greatly befriended the fugitive king and his followers, by bringing them wheat and barley, and flour, and parched corn, and sheep, and honey, and mats for covering by night. When Absalom was slain, and David returned to Jerusalem, he took with him Chimham, the son of old Barzillai, and treated him like a child at his own table; and subsequently gave him his own house, which he had inherited from his father Jesse, at Bethlehem. And when David was dying, in his last words, he charged Solomon, his son and successor, to be kind to Chimham, and to ensure to him the possession of the house in Bethlehem, where Ruth lived and David himself was born.

Four hundred and thirty years afterwards, in the days of Jeremiah the prophet, when

Jerusalem was in ruins, and the tribes of Israel had been carried captive to Babylon, the strong stone-built house, given by king David to the son of his benefactor, was still standing in Bethlehem, and it was still called the house of Chimham. It had then become the khan, or public house of the village. Jeremiah himself took refuge within its walls, when his friend and protector Gedaliah, the deputy governor appointed by the king of Babylon, had been treacherously slain at Mizpeh, a few miles north of Jerusalem.

At that time, a great company of fugitives, also fearing the wrath of Nebuchadnezzar for the murder of his governor, came down from Gibeon and filled the whole house of Chimham, and encamped upon the slopes of the hill and in the open spaces of the town. Jeremiah, speaking by the word of the Lord, warned them to go back to their homes and fear nothing. But they disobeyed and passed on in the other direction into Egypt, taking the prophet himself with them, and there they all died.

Five hundred and eighty years pass, and

Bethlehem, with the Road to Jerusalem in Foreground.

light breaks again upon the house of Chimham, the khan of Bethlehem where Ruth lived and David was born, and Jeremiah received the word of the Lord. It is still the public caravanserai of the town, and two weary travelers from the hills of Nazareth come at a late hour, through the whole length of the straggling street, to the eastern extremity of the town, to seek rest and shelter for the night in this ancient and historic abode on the brow of the hill.

The open area within the walls is all covered with men, women and children; horses, asses and camels, sleeping promiscuously together upon the stone floor. The narrow, doorless, unfurnished stalls or sleeping chambers in the walls, opening under arches upon a raised piazza round three sides of the area, are all full. The late travelers are obliged to seek shelter outside of the inner wall of the caravanserai, beneath archways extending back under the projecting and cavernous rocks of the hill-side, and used only for the protection of servants, muleteers and animals in bad weather. "There is no room" for these benighted late comers "in the inn." The sides of this outer enclosure are fitted up with mangers built into the walls, with small stones and mortar, and shaped like a kneading trough.

In such a dismal, stony, unfurnished, windowless, doorless cell was the Redeemer of the world born. In such a rude, stone-built manger was the babe lying when the shepherds, watching their flocks in the fields below the town, heard the angel voice, saying, "Behold, I bring you good tidings of great joy, which shall be unto all people. For unto you is born this day, in the city of David, a Saviour, which is Christ, the Lord."

And the joy was too great for a single messenger to bring from heaven to earth. For suddenly the whole plain seemed to have become camping ground for the angelic host, and a multitude of voices broke forth in the song which all the nations shall yet learn to sing—"Glory to God in the highest, and on earth peace, good-will to men." And when the angels ceased and departed, the shepherds ran with haste, climbed up the hill-side among terraced gardens and evergreen olives and came to the stable of the inn, and found, as the angel had said, "the babe lying in a manger."

Thenceforth the house of David on the brow of that hill, is consecrated in all Christian memories forevermore. Fruitful, vine-clad Bethlehem, which signifies "the house of bread," becomes the representative of that living Bread which came down from heaven, of which, if a man partake, he shall never die. Contentious, war-loving Bethlehem sends forth a song of peace which shall be sung in all the languages of men, and shall resound through all the ages of time. Royal, king-nursing Bethlehem, becomes the birth-place of a Prince whose glory shall fill the earth, and whose dominion shall endure throughout all generations. Proud, beautiful Bethlehem, nestled among hills and smiling on the desert, sends forth a message of mercy, to comfort all that mourn, to lift up all that are cast down and to gladden all the waste places of the earth.

The story of Bethlehem loses nothing of its

meaning or its power with the progress of time. It never meant so much in the minds of men as it does now, and it will hold a higher place in human history, when it is thirty-six centuries old, than it does now, when it is eighteen.

It is impossible for us to describe, or to imagine, the depths of humiliation to which the Son of God subjected himself, in accomplishing the work of our redemption. We may call to our aid the utmost resources of reason and imagination, supposition and argument, and yet we shall fail to measure the distance between the throne of heaven and the manger of Bethlehem. And yet it becomes us to avail ourselves of every expedient and suggestion, which may help us to dwell on the mighty theme, till our minds are lost in wonder, love and adoration. To this end indulge a single supposition.

Suppose it to have been told in heaven that the fulness of the prophetic times had come, the great expiation for man's sin was about to be made, the Son of God had already appeared incarnate on earth; and some ministering angel, just returned from a mission of love to some far distant world, hastens down to be present at the sacrifice. He has seen the glory which the eternal Son had with the Father before the world was. He has bowed with veiled face in the presence of the unapproachable Light. He naturally supposes that the Lord of angels and the Son of the Highest, will be attended with a retinue commensurate with the dignity of his divine nature, even when offering himself to bear an infinite weight of suffering for man's sin. He is prepared to witness the assemblage of all nations, at some great imperial capital. He expects nothing less than that the divine Messiah will be surrounded by legions of angels, and that he will receive the visible homage of cherub and of burning seraphim, in the very moment of his mysterious agony, that the world may believe in his greatness when beholding his glory.

With such expectations, the inquiring angel approaches our earth. But he sees it illumined with no unusual light. He hears no sounds of exultant joy from the race whom the Son of God had come to save. He has learned something of a chosen people; of a city where Jehovah had placed his name; of a temple which had been hallowed for ages by awful symbols of the divine presence. He directs his flight to Jerusalem; hovers in mid-air over the mount of Zion. But he sees no signs of the august ceremony there.

The proud priests are offering polluted sacrifice in the temple. The prouder Pharisees are addressing the multitude, in the courts of the Lord's house and at the corners of the streets, vociferating long prayers, displaying the precepts of the law and the traditions of the elders inwoven upon their garments, and worn in phylacteries upon their foreheads. The armor of the Roman soldier clanks at every gate, upon every tower and wall. The inquiring angel sees no evidence of the Redeemer's presence, in the city, where the daily sacrifice for a thousand years had promised his coming and typified his death.

Could it be that the Son of God, to draw the attention of all nations, had chosen to make his advent at the capital of the world's great empire? Alas! the imperial city on the banks of the Tiber, is in no mood to welcome the Redeemer of mankind. From the marble seats of the amphitheatre, a hundred thousand spectators look down with eager and savage joy upon human combatants cutting each other to pieces, "to make a Roman holiday." When one falls beneath the more dexterous sword of his antagonist, and his life blood stains the trampled sand of the arena, the acclamation from the crowded galleries, rises loud as the shout of nations, hoarse and horrible as the roar of the deep in storms.

In another quarter, the congregated wisdom of the Roman Senate is voting divine honors to the cruel and beastly despot, who has gratified the passions of the populace, with such murderous amusement. Surely, in such a city, the heavenly visitant finds little evidence of a disposition to rejoice at the coming of the Prince of peace.

Nor would he find a better preparation for the promised Messiah, should he turn to Athens, "the eye of Greece," the fountain of learning and philosophy, the home of the arts, the haunt of the muses. The Greeks are too busy with the fables of false gods, to welcome a new revelation from the only wise and true.

And the great capitals of ancient empire, Thebes, Babylon, Nineveh, had been levelled with the dust long before, by the judgments of heaven executed upon their crimes. The bird of night, and the beast of prey, had found a home, amid the desolate palaces of Egypt's kings, and the fallen temples of Assyrian gods.

Wearied with the fruitless search for the scene of the divine incarnation, the inquiring angel begins to suspect that he has mistaken the world, in which the great expiation was about to be made. Shocked and terrified by the universal prevalence and boundless excesses of misery and crime, he begins to fear that he has alighted upon the region of the outcast and accursed. He is just about to wing his way back, when suddenly he sees, almost beneath him, to the south of Jerusalem, the whole air ablaze with gathering myriads of the heavenly host. He hears the chorus of blest voices, proclaiming the tidings that Christ is born in the city of David, and that his earthly abode is with the beasts of the stall.

And there indeed was the Son of God, the Redeemer of the world, in all outward appearance as frail and helpless as the creatures whom he was born to save. If angels ministered unto him, they were not permitted to display their glory before the eyes of men; they must not sing his praise in songs that could be heard by ears of flesh and blood. If the swift messengers of the skies bore the tidings of his birth with joy to the courts of heaven, no such intelligence was announced in the palaces of earthly monarchs; shepherds were told of the coming of the King of glory, while princes and philosophers knew it not.

The proud Pharisee, with hypocritical devotion, courting the homage of the superstitious rabble in the streets of Jerusalem; the learned Rabbi, expounding the law in the schools of the prophets, knew nothing of the Babe in the manger of Bethlehem. Their Messiah was to be an earthly prince, who should reign on the throne of David and crush the heathen with his conquering arm, not the despised Nazarene who should suffer and die. The great and mighty of the earth, who were devising schemes to perpetuate their own dominion to the latest posterity, made no account of that

Prince whose throne should be set up in millions of hearts, and whose kingdom should endure forever and ever.

And who could have supposed that the King of glory would stoop so low? Who could have thought that the divine nature would shroud itself in the frail form of a child, whose lowly bed was made in a manger? Who would dare say that angels might bow down and worship before that babe, without forfeiting their allegiance to the King of heaven? What prophet would have been believed in Bethlehem, if he had said of the son of Mary, " He shall feed the destitute by thousands, yet himself suffer the pangs of hunger; he shall supply consolation for the most afflicted, yet himself become preëminently the Man of sorrows; he shall be holy, harmless, undefiled, separate from sin, yet on him shall be laid the iniquities of us all; he shall still the tempest with a word, yet himself want protection from heat and cold; he shall give rest to the weary and heavy-laden, yet himself not have where to lay his head; he shall heal the sick with the touch of his hand, yet himself be as sensitive to bodily pain as they; he shall cast out devils, yet himself be assailed by the temptations of Satan; he shall raise the dead by his own power, yet himself suffer the pangs of death."

He might, indeed, have astonished the world by a display of his real person, clothed in the splendors with which he shone in the highest heaven. He might have revealed himself at the very first in flaming fire, attended by ten thousand thousand of his ministering spirits. He might have descended from above upon Mount Zion, with the trump of the archangel to herald his coming, and the wing of cherubim to waft his flying throne. But he made himself of no reputation, and took upon him the form of a servant, and it is only because he submitted to such humiliation, that we have the hope of glory and immortality.

And shall not this wonderful story of Bethlehem teach us to pour contempt on all our human pride? The Son of God consents to be a stranger. And shall men complain that they are unappreciated or unknown? The King of glory takes the form of a servant, and shall men complain that their condition is lowly and their honors few? The strength of omnipotence clothed itself with the feebleness of a child; the hand that spread out the heavens and laid the foundation of the earth, appeared as the hand of a babe needing to be led, waiting to be lifted up. And shall any humiliation seem to us too deep, if in our lowly estate we can have the sympathy and companionship of One who made the worlds and holds the stars in his right hand?

The story of Bethlehem shows us how deep is the divine sympathy with us in all the walks of life. In illustrating this first page of gospel history, we must speak of humble homes, and comfortless houses, and weary journeys, and laborious occupations, and meagre living, and rude garments, and cheerless apartments, and jostlings with strangers and lodging with cattle. And in all these places and experiences, the divine Life dwells with men. They are all embraced and sanctified in the earthly history of the incarnate Son of God that we may learn to cherish the holiest purposes in the humblest occupations, that we may make all the trials and toils and experiences of life, the means of bringing us into higher communion with our Maker.

Barns and brute cattle should be dedicated to God, since Jesus was laid in a manger. Poor, hard-working laborers may be the especial favorites of heaven, since angels bore the best tidings that ever came to this world, first to shepherds. Hotels and taverns may be made holy places, since wise men of the East found the Saviour of the world in a caravanserai. The most unwelcome exactions may bring us blessings, since it was in consequence of the edict of the taxgatherer, that Bethlehem became the birthplace of Christ. All the beautiful things of art, and all the precious things of wealth, and all the sacred things of affection may be dedicated to Christ, since gold and frankincense and myrrh were offered to the infant Saviour, even before his glory was manifested before the world. The Son of God in his humiliation passed through all the depths and necessities of our lowly estate that he might sanctify all departments of human life and teach us to live for God in them all.

The story of Bethlehem is one of great joy to all people. It is joy to the poor; for Christ comes to make them heirs of the kingdom of God. It is joy to the rich; for Christ comes to teach them how to use all their earthly possessions, so as to lay up for themselves imperishable riches in heaven. It is joy to the ignorant; for Christ comes to make them wise unto eternal salvation. It is joy to the learned; for Christ comes to unfold mysteries that have been kept secret from the foundation of the world. It is joy to the mourning and the comfortless; for Christ comes to heal all sorrow, and to bind up every broken heart. It is joy to the guilty, the condemned and the despairing; for Christ comes to take away transgression, to bear the sins of many and to give himself a ransom for the world. The wave of joy, flowing forth from the angel-song of Bethlehem, is wide enough to encompass the earth, and rich enough to bless every human soul, and deep enough to flow on through all coming time.

The story of Bethlehem is worthy to be received with faith, and gratitude, and joy by every heart. All the events of past history taken together, are of less consequence to us, than the single fact that the Son of God became incarnate, suffered and died for our salvation. All the researches of science, all the reasonings of philosophy, all the inventions of genius, have not poured so much light upon the world as the star that led to the place where Christ was born. The highest and longest enjoyment of health, the acquisition of millions of money, success in all worldly enterprises, were nothing like so great an occasion for gratitude and joy as is given us all by the knowledge of the glory of God as it shines in the face of Jesus Christ.

Oh! when shall earth's uncounted millions join the angel host in singing for joy that Christ was born in Bethlehem? When shall all for whom the Saviour died, accept with grateful faith, this awful and merciful mystery of the divine incarnation, as the greatest event in the history of time—When shall the one song of "Peace on earth, and glory in the Highest," employ all nations?

> "The dwellers in the vales and on the rocks
> Shout to each other, and the mountain tops
> From distant mountains catch the flying joy;
> Till nation after nation taught the strain,
> Earth rolls the rapturous hosanna round?"

The song of angels, which proclaimed the coming of the Son of God on earth, had scarcely ceased upon the plain of Bethlehem,' when the wrath of man broke forth for the defeat of the purposed mercy, and the destruction of the infant Saviour. The Babe, whose birth was an occasion of joy to the heavenly host, soon became the subject of suspicion and rage to the rulers of the earth. Out of the city of David, out of the Land of Promise, beyond the realm of kings who reigned in his own Jerusalem, beyond the reach of priests who ministered in his own temple of Zion, must the infant Messiah be borne, or the earth would lose its Saviour, and the stream of salvation be dried at the fountain.

He who came to be the Light of the world, must be carried away by night and hidden from the world in the land of darkness. The divine Deliverer of Israel, and of the nations, must go down to Egypt and dwell in the house of bondage, before he can be permitted to proclaim liberty to the captives, and the opening of the prison to them that are bound.

Of that long and lonely pilgrimage, which began by night at Bethlehem, and continued for many days over the waste of Arabian deserts, and ended in the deeper night and worse desolation of exile in Egypt, we know nothing. But it is much to know that the holy child Jesus was a fugitive for his life in his infancy, and that the divine Saviour, when his glory was fully manifested before the world, was crucified in his death.

NAZARETH.

He came to Nazareth where he had been brought up.- LUKE iv. 16.

II.

NAZARETH.

AFTER the wondrous birth in Bethlehem, and the hurried flight into Egypt, the strange story of the divine incarnation returns to the secluded spot where it began, among the hills of Galilee. The Son of God has appeared upon the great mission of redemption, announced as king and Messiah by a multitude of the heavenly host, and yet he must be hidden from the world thirty years before he makes himself known. For so long a time he must live by toil, in dependence and obscurity, as if he were the least of the sons of men. For a whole generation he must shut the great secret of his work and character in his own heart, teaching first the long, hard lesson of silence, and patience, and waiting, that he may be heard the more gladly by the poor and the "common people," when he speaks.

In regard to the precise manner in which Jesus spent the years of man's life, from childhood to mature age, the sacred writers maintain the most profound and solemn reserve. The irreverent and inquisitive spirit of later times, has endeavored to lift the awful veil with which inspiration covers the home and the occupations of the child and the man Jesus before his manifestation to the world. But all such attempts have only served to impress us more fully with the wisdom of the divine purpose, which has shrouded this early period in the life of the incarnate Son of God in impenetrable mystery. Mercy has communicated all that can help our faith, and wisdom has withholden what would only supply materials for the employment of a profane and profitless curiosity.

Nevertheless we are told the place where Jesus was "brought up," the obscure mountain village where the Saviour of the world was hidden from the eyes of men for so many years. And it is becoming in us to manifest a profound interest in the secluded spot where the divine "Child grew and waxed strong in spirit, and increased in wisdom and stature, and in favor with God and man." From that humble home in Nazareth there has gone forth a power which has already encompassed the earth, and is destined to sway the sceptre of supreme command over all nations.

Nazareth was written upon the cross in the three great languages which gave law, art and religion to the world; and the name shall be associated with everything that rules, refines and consecrates the human race, long as faith finds a home on the earth, long as Christ has a kingdom in the hearts of men.

The despised name of the place and the people has been ascribed to the greatest achievements and possessions of man, and it is still borne and accepted by Him, who sits upon the throne of heaven. Such a village, however small and remote and despised, may well awaken our most rational and devout curiosity.

The double range of Lebanon diminishes in height, and divides into waving ridges or rounded hills, as it approaches the great plain of Esdraelon. Here and there, the mountain mass separates for a little space on the surface, and then unites and flows on as the water of a swift-running stream, divided by a jutting rock, unites again at a little distance below the obstacle, and then flows on at its former level, leaving a hollow space between the point of separation and of union. In such a narrow,

depressed valley, a mile long and high up above the plain, and walled in by still higher hills stands the little town whose existence was not known in history till it became the home of Jesus, but whose name has now been carried to the ends of the earth.

The road to Jerusalem which the Holy Family traveled every year going and returning, climbs up from the plain over a long, steep staircase of rocky ledges and loosened stones, where the sure-footed Syrian horses fear to climb, and the bravest riders feel safer on their feet. Having attained a ridge half as high as Tabor, the rugged path descends into a secluded and peaceful vale, on the south-western side of which stands Nazareth.

The name was thought to signify "place of flowers." And the name was well chosen, whether the meaning referred to the millions of flowers strewn through the valley, or to the appearance of the little white town itself, resting in the cup of the one colossal flower, of which the fifteen encompassing hills are the green petals to enhance its beauty and to protect it from danger. The soil of the enclosed basin is fertile and well cultivated. Gardens and corn-fields, green hedges and barren foot-paths, clusters of orange and pomegranate, olive and fig-trees diversify the plain and adorn the hillsides. The white rocks and gray, bare ledges that stand out here and there upon the slopes and upper ridges of the hills, afford a pleasing and impressive contrast with the green hollows and cultivated grounds below. Walled in and sheltered on every side from blighting winds and sudden changes, the valley enjoys a mild and equable climate, and brings forth fruit and grain, the first and best of the country and the season.

The traveler who crosses the great battle plain of Esdraelon, reviving its memories of blood as he rides for hours through a waving sea of verdure, and then climbs the steep and rocky defile to the edge of the basin of Nazareth, and looks down through thickets of vines and groves of fig and olive trees, upon the quiet town and the cultivated gardens, feels, for the moment, that he has alighted upon a "happy valley," where the pride and conflict of the world can never come. He imagines the peaceful inhabitants of this secluded vale climbing the natural rampart with which they are surrounded, and looking forth with horror on plundered fields and burning towns, and slaughtered people around Tabor and Gilboa and Megiddo, and rejoicing that the wasteful passions which make man a wolf to man have never been kindled in their quiet homes. He thinks that here at last, out of the track of great armies, afar from the vices and corruptions of great cities in happy ignorance of the pomp and pride of the great world, truth may speak upon every lip, virtue adorn every home, peace dwell in every heart.

Alas! that the first page in the history of this mountain village, and the first hour's experience within its present streets, should dissipate so pleasant a dream. No mountain walls can shut out the enemy that found entrance at the gates of Paradise. No seclusion from the world can exempt individuals or families from that mortal contagion which began with the first sin, and still runs in the blood of all the race. The people of Nazareth had a bad reputation even among the Galileans, the rudest and worst of the people of Palestine; and the residence of Jesus in the little town for thirty years did not make it any better.

How significant and awful the humiliation of the Son of God, that he should consent to live for so many years unhonored, unknown, in this rude, despised and wicked town. It would have been infinite condescension in him to have lived, for a single year, in the holiest place or. earth; or to have maintained the state of kings in the most gorgeous palace ever built by human hands; or to have received the gifts and homage of all nations, while every tongue and every language was burdened with his praise.

But for thirty years he dwelt in a town from which it was thought a wonder if any good thing should come; he passed his daily life with a people whose treatment of him warranted the bad reputation which their neighbors gave them. He began his mighty work of lifting the whole human race up from darkness and misery by going down himself to that condition which the proud world despises and tramples upon. He set his own feet upon the paths which the poor and neglected must tread. He took to his own bosom the woes which the afflicted must suffer. He lived thirty years of his life in this depraved and despised Nazareth, that he might pour silent contempt upon the world's pride of place, and fortune, and fame. He passed by the renowned seats of wisdom, and glory, and empire, and made his home in this humble, mountain village, that his followers might learn to make any post of duty honorable by their own greatness and fidelity.

It will take all the centuries of time, and the ages of eternity to measure the distinction which the name of Jesus has conferred upon this despised Nazareth. Everything which meets the eye within this narrow vale is associated forever with him, whose work shall become the song of all nations, and whose glory shall fill the earth and the heavens. To some humble home in this quiet vale, Gabriel, "the mighty one of God," was sent to bear the best tidings ever brought from heaven to earth,— tidings that the Prince, the Son of the Highest, of whom the same heavenly messenger had spoken to Daniel the prophet, five hundred years before, was about to appear. To this calm retreat the infant Saviour came back from the flight into Egypt.

Breathing this air, drinking of these fountains, eating of the fruit of these gardens, living in a home just like one of these white stone houses, he grew from infancy to manhood. Through these narrow streets, along these winding field-paths, up and down these terraced hill-sides, up and down the steep and stony road, from the great plain to the mountain valley, he passed as peasants now pass to their morning toil and their evening rest. He listened to the birds of the air, the lark, the linnet, the nightingale and the turtle dove, whose voices are now heard in this valley. He delighted himself with the wild flowers that still make the meadows glow with their beauty. This dome of sky spread over him with the brightness of noon, with the glory of clouds, and sunsets, and stars. These everlasting hills offered him their solitudes for a sanctuary. These wild olive groves, beyond the cultivated fields, covered him with their shadows when he spent the night alone in communion with his Father. These dark glens heard his voice when he went out before the dawn to pray. From these lofty heights he looked forth upon a land that waited a thousand years for his

Little Hermon. Shunem. Mt. Gilboa. Hills of Samaria.

coming, and received him not when he came. From the rocky walls, reared without hands around this mountain home, he refreshed his spirit in the morning wind from the great sea, over which his Gospel should be carried to nations and continents then unknown.

We do not indeed know the precise spot on which the home of Jesus stood. We cannot tell which one of these many paths among the gardens and vineyards was trodden by his feet. We speak only from strong probability when we say that the child Jesus must have often gone forth to this fountain in company with the blessed mother. But it is certain that his home was in this quiet vale, and that the little town, "where he was brought up," is still here. And that alone is enough to make the valley of Nazareth, with all its permanent natural features, sacred forevermore in the memory of all who believe that Jesus is indeed the Son of God.

The treatment which our Lord received when he attempted to begin his public ministry at Nazareth, is a sad and fearful exhibition of the worst passions of the human heart.

He had been baptized in Jordan and proclaimed by a voice from heaven as the Son of God. He had triumphed in a three-fold conflict with the Prince of darkness. He had manifested forth his glory by mighty works and divine instructions at Cana, at Capernaum and at Jerusalem. He had returned to the secluded home where he had lived so long, teaching and performing miracles as he came from town to town, in the synagogues, in the streets, on the hill-sides, by the sea-shore; wherever the people would gather to hear, wherever the sick were brought to be healed.

His fame had gone before him and his return awakened curiosity in Nazareth itself. But he was received with so much distrust and jealousy, that even he who had lived with the people thirty years, "marvelled at their unbelief." He went about their streets, and talked with the people, and laid his hands on a few sick persons and healed them. But he was everywhere met with jealous eyes and contemptuous words. The members of his own family thought he was "beside himself," and few could be found having faith enough to receive aid from his healing power.

When the Sabbath came, he went in and took his seat in the synagogue, as he had been accustomed to do in former years. The service of song and prayer and reading the scriptures and exhortation was administered by the chief elder in the usual form. At the close of the service, when the attendant of the synagogue was carrying back the book of the prophet Isaiah, from the pulpit in the centre of the house, to the ark at the end towards Jerusalem and all eyes were fixed with awe upon the sacred scroll, Jesus stood up as he could do according to the usage of the service, and demanded that the scroll should be given him to read. Unrolling the parchment and standing there, himself the living and divine interpreter of the prophet's words, he read, "The Spirit of the Lord is upon me; because he hath anointed me to preach the gospel to the poor; he hath sent me to heal the brokenhearted, to preach deliverance to the captives, and recovering of sight to the blind, and to set at liberty those that are bruised, to preach the acceptable year of the Lord."

It was a great occasion for the little town of Nazareth, when Jesus read those words in their synagogue and said, "This day is this scripture fulfilled in your ears." It was the first time that he had publicly declared himself to be the ANOINTED of the Lord. None of the prophets or kings or judges in the whole line of Jewish history had ventured to assume that exalted and awful name the MESSIAH. Leaving the Holy City, and all the sacred and renowned places in the land, and all the wise and mighty among the people behind, he had come to this rude and despised mountain village to speak, for the first time, the greatest and the most gracious words that had ever been spoken on earth. In this humble synagogue of Nazareth, he had made the declaration which the faithful in Israel had waited and longed for ages and for centuries to hear, and had died without the sound.

Oh! happy city, to whom the Prince of peace himself brings the message of salvation. First in opportunity, be thou first to welcome the world's Redeemer, and all nations shall call thee blessed. Let thy voice break forth in the first hosannas to the Lord's Anointed, and streams of salvation shall flow from thy favored valley to all lands, and pilgrims from the ends of the earth, shall come to walk in the shadow of thy mountains and to worship on the spot where Christ received the first homage of a ransomed world.

Alas! for unhappy, unbelieving Nazareth, that the rare opportunity to attain such exalted, such blessed distinction should be worse than thrown away. The eyes of all in the synagogue were fastened upon Jesus when he claimed that this great Messianic prophecy was fulfilled in him. Their astonishment knew no bounds. They had seen Jesus a child in their streets. His home was among the poor; he had pursued an humble and laborious occupation for years. His family had never gained the distinction of learning, or riches, or rank, or power. They were looking for a Messiah who should come with the state of a king and the glory of a conqueror. He must appear at the head of armies, and his legions must fly as the clouds. He must tread down the heathen in his wrath, and deliver Israel from every yoke.

Such an one will Nazareth receive as the anointed of the Lord, not this son of Mary, this brother of James, and Joses, and Jude, who had been known among them as a carpenter for twenty years. The very humiliation which our blessed Lord had taken upon himself in love for our lost race, and which should have opened every heart to receive him, was an offense to the rude and passionate people with whom he had lived so long.

He had promised the kingdom of heaven to the poor. They only desired him to bestow the riches and honors of a kingdom on earth. He had come to heal those who were brokenhearted for their sins. They were not looking for such consolation as can be attained only through penitence and contrition of soul. He had preached deliverance to those who were held captive by Satan. They were more anxious to be delivered from bondage to Cæsar. He had come in meekness and lowliness, in poverty and sorrow. They wanted riches and splendor; the parade of monarchs, and the trumpets of victory.

And so they cried out against him with wrath and cursing. Out of their synagogue, out of their city, out of the world would they cast him whose only offense was the meekness and plainness with which he had spoken the truth. The favored people, who were the first to hear the most gracious words from the lips of Christ himself, were the first to cry, "away with him." With one consent, and with deafening cries, they break up the assembly; they surround him; they lay hands upon him, every one eager to bear a part in destroying him; they hurry him forth to the brow of a precipice, near by the synagogue, that they may cast him down headlong. But suddenly when they looked for him, he was not there. He had passed through the midst of them and was gone. He was not unwilling to die, even for their redemption; but the hour for the sacrifice had not yet come. They had had the opportunity to secure the greatest distinction ever conferred on any town or city since the world began, and they had rejected it.

In the course of the following winter, he came once more, and for the last time, to this secluded vale of Nazareth, after the people had had time to reflect and to repent of their madness. He came when the fame of his mighty works had filled the whole land. He had silenced and cast out demons with his word. The sick had been brought to him out of all Galilee, and he had healed them. He had given sight to the blind, and hearing to the deaf, and speech to the dumb. At Capernaum and at the neighboring hill-town of Nain, he had raised the dead to life. And these evidences of his divine power had been witnessed by thousands. And the name of Nazareth had gone with him through all the land.

But still the blinded and fanatical Nazarenes could see nothing but a carpenter in the son of Mary. Having once committed themselves to the rejection of Jesus, it was still too much for their pride to recognise in him the promised Redeemer of Israel, the Saviour of the world. And so Nazareth confirmed and fastened on itself forever the dreadful reputation of having been the first to receive the public

NAZARETH. 63

announcement of the Messiah from his own lips, and the first to reject him.

The evidences that Jesus of Nazareth is the Son of God and the only Saviour, have been increasing from century to century, for eighteen hundred years, and still there are millions to reject him. He comes to the weary with the offer of rest, and they cling to their burdens and refuse his help. He comes to the afflicted, offering to heal their sorrows and bear their grief, and they still mourn over their troubles and will not be comforted. He comes to the worldly and the unbelieving, to the disappointed and the unhappy, offering to do for them just what they need most to have done, bringing the testimony of millions on earth and in heaven, that he is able to do all that he promises. And yet they shut their hearts against him; they live without peace, and they die without hope.

When Jesus shall come in his glory, the men of Nazareth will pray to be covered by the rocks of their own mountains, rather than meet the face of him whom they thrust out of their synagogue, and would have hurled down the precipice of their hill-side. Still greater in that day will be the consternation of those who have had the history of Christianity for two thousand years and the testimony of millions on earth and in heaven to help their faith, and yet have not believed.

It is indeed human to err, and the wisest often mistake. But all other mistakes are as nothing compared with the one of rejecting Christ. All have sinned, and if God should be strict to mark iniquity against us, we could not answer him for one of a thousand of our transgressions. And all other sins may be forgiven. But for him who rejects Christ, there is no other Saviour. To reject him is to reject infinite love, infinite truth, infinite mercy. To turn him from the heart is to renounce all of life, and peace, and joy, that heaven and eternity have in store for the redeemed soul. To reject Christ is to say, "Prison of despair be my habitation; Prince of darkness, reign over me forever."

CAPERNAUM.

Leaving Nazareth, He came and dwelt in Capernaum.—
MATT. iv. 13.

III.
CAPERNAUM.

SEA OF TIBERIAS.

AT Bethlehem, Jesus was born, at Nazareth, he was brought up, at Jerusalem, he died. Capernaum enjoys the rare distinction of being called "his own city." At Capernaum alone, he is said to have been "at home." Expelled from their synagogue and from their streets by the rude and fanatical dwellers among the hills, he came down to the lake-side to make his abode and begin his ministry.

The little sea of Galilee fills the bed of a volcanic rift among the highlands. The waters from the hills have run down and filled the mouth of the furnace out of which the earth-fires once flamed. The steam, rising from hot and sulphurous fountains flowing across the white beach at the southern extremity, proves that the fires are still burning beneath. The lake looks the less in size because it lies so deep between the parted hills, and the clearness of the atmosphere brings the encompassing walls so near each other.

When the sky is clear, and the sun is high at noon, and the scathed and furrowed cliffs cast no shadows upon the still surface of the water, the whole landscape has a blasted and desolate expression, as if lying under the spell of some awful doom. But the whole scene is changed when the day breaks with the glory of an eastern dawn over the hills of Bashan, or the evening casts its purple shadows from Tabor and the mount of the Beatitudes, or a sudden blast rushes down through the wild gorges of the high table-lands, and lashes the whole surface of the lake into snow-white foam. Travelers, who only ride down from the hills of Galilee and spend a hot and weary day in traversing the white beach, gazing upon the glimmering sand, the glassy waters, and the brown shore, are apt to pronounce the whole scene desolate, monotonous and uninteresting. But those who take time to witness the changes of calm and storm, morning and evening, noon and night, never tire of talking of its beauty.

The whole region has greatly changed since Jesus came down from Nazareth to make his new home at Capernaum. Then the lake was alive with boats, scudding before the wind, moving slow with laboring oars, or resting in the calm with drooping sails. The white line of the shore was set with bright little towns, like a string of pearls encased between the edge of the burnished mirror and its brown frame-work of hills. Villages of white stone houses covered the neighboring heights; hamlets clustered on the terraced slopes, and at the head of valleys looking toward the lake. The sower cast his seed into all the good ground of the narrow plain, and the vintager trained his vines wherever earth enough could be found to hold the root on the sunny cliffs and ledges.

The deep depression of the lake acted upon the enclosed air like some vast conservatory, keeping up a tropical temperature through most of the year. Flowers blossomed and fruits ripened on the shores, while the snow lay in sight on the hills above. The fishermen boasted that they drank the waters of the Nile and enjoyed the climate of Egypt, while the shepherds were shivering with cold on the neighboring heights, or were wandering from valley to valley in search of fountains for their thirsty flocks. The green band lying between the white beach and the base of the hills, was crossed and fertilized in many places by streams bursting forth with a river's strength, from the foot of the cliffs. In one place this narrow band widened to a breadth of several miles, forming a plain which received the name of Gennesaret,—"Gardens of Princes,"—"Paradise." Near the northern boundary of this fertile plain was the town where Jesus came to make his home.

Capernaum was but one of nine cities standing directly upon the lake-shore, the whole circuit of which could be seen from the roof of the synagogue which the Roman centurion had built, and in which Jesus often taught. From the same point, numerous high places could be seen on the Galilean shore, crowned with villages, the least of which was large enough to be called a city; beautiful, as all eastern towns are beautiful in the distance; shining with their white stone houses, like alabaster in the morning sun, and all crowded with a restless and busy population. During the day, pleasure boats were darting to and fro upon the whole surface of the lake, and at evening, hundreds of fishermen put forth to let down their nets and gather of every kind.

Jesus did not go down to Capernaum to seek retirement, or to find a quiet and cultivated people. The town was in the very focus of all social and industrial activity in northern Palestine. The region was more densely peopled than any other portion of the country, and the population was more various than elsewhere. Jew, Greek and Roman mingled with Arab,

Persian and Egyptian, in the streets of the ten cities, and in the trade of the miniature sea. The only carriage roads ever made in Palestine were built by the Romans, and the most important of them all passed through Capernaum from Damascus to Jerusalem. Pilgrims, merchants, caravans, scholars, laborers, devotees, were continually passing north and south. The words spoken by Jesus on the Mount of the Beatitudes within sight of the city, and the mighty works done by him in its streets, would soon be reported in Syria and Arabia, in Greece and Egypt, as well as in all Palestine.

The great Teacher bound up his sacred precepts with all the peculiar seasons, aspects and occupations of the region; and he put forth his divine power to help and to heal Jew, Greek and Roman; the rich who were courted for their wealth, and the poor who were despised for their poverty; the leprous whom everybody shunned, and the possessed whom everybody feared. So, taking his stand where the stream of the world's travel passed between east and west, north and south, Babylon and Rome, Scythia and Ethiopia, speaking to instruct, and putting forth his hand to help all that went and came, Jesus presented himself as the Saviour of men, the Desired of all nations, the bond of union between all kindreds and tribes of the earth. His peculiar mode of teaching in the synagogue of Capernaum, on the shore of the lake, and on the hill-sides above the city, has the stamp of reality in every illustration, and it has graven the leading features of the scene upon the minds of millions who were never there.

1. THE SEA-SIDE.

The time that Jesus abode in Capernaum is divided into nine periods of sojourn in the city, and nine of missionary excursions through the neighboring towns and districts. Four times we find him teaching by the lake-side, three times in the synagogue, once on the mount above the city, and always speaking the words of eternal life, as he came and went up and down the wild paths of the hill-country, as he entered into hamlets and villages, crossed and recrossed the lake, dined and lodged with rich and poor and made himself equally familiar with all the interests and occupations of men.

By his blessed life and mighty works and divine instructions, he made the lake, the shore, the hills, the sky, hallowed in the hearts of his followers for all succeeding time. By reviving, so far as we can, scenes in the midst of which he lived and walked with men, we give reality to our faith, we bring the divine and human into closer relations with each other, we make it easier to believe that even now, the humblest home may receive the Son of God for a guest, the lowliest occupation may be of service to him.

Let us go down to the lake-side and listen, while Jesus speaks to the fishermen on the shore. It is the morning hour, and the flush of dawn is kindling and rising along the level wall of the eastern mountains. The hills, the shore, the white towns, the oak woods of Tabor and the barren heights of Bashan rise to view with increasing clearness, and above, the stars, that hung all night like crystal lamps from the blue dome of the sky, go out, one by one, in the coming glory of the full day. The still surface of the lake lies like a dark mirror of burnished steel encased in its high frame-work

evening to conversation, the night to sleep. And now in Capernaum, travelers are starting on their journey, laborers are going out to work in the fields and vineyards, merchantmen are pursuing their trade, women are bringing water from fountains, shepherds are leading forth their flocks on the hills, and fishermen are gathering upon the shore.

Jesus is no longer alone. The toilers upon the sea signal to each other, that the Prophet of Nazareth may be seen on the shore, and laboring oars are pulling in boats from every direction. The multitudes, who had followed Jesus from the hill-country and had lodged in the town over night, have learned his retreat, and are hurrying down to the beach, carrying with them as many more from the streets of Capernaum. The surging crowd gather closer and closer upon Jesus until he is pressed down to the water's edge. At last he is compelled to request one of the fishermen to receive him into his boat, and thrust out a little from the land, that the people may no longer tread upon each other in the endeavor to approach him, and that they may the better give quiet attention to his words.

And so he sits in the bow of the unsteady boat, teaching the multitude that stand or recline and listen on the shore. Calm, patient, condescending, he bears with their rudeness, he pities their ignorance, he speaks to them as man never spake.

Oh! what a scene is this. The Son of God, the King of heaven, the Sovereign of all worlds, comes upon a mission of mercy for the redemption of nations, and he passes by the schools of philosophy, the courts of kings, the camp of the conqueror, and he goes down to the lake-side, in the early morning, to deliver his message to peasants and fishermen. He sits there upon the swaying seat of a fisherman's boat, talking to the rude and noisy crowd on the shore, when he might sit upon the throne of heaven, and receive the homage of archangels.

And in this humble scene on the shore of the Galilean lake, we find the most momentous crisis in human destiny. Under the calm deportment of this unpretending teacher, who came down from the hills of Nazareth, is treasured up the germ of revolutions and conquests, heroisms and sacrifices which shall make a new history for the world. With his gentle words there shall go forth a power to stir and shake the nations, as the lake is roused and ploughed into foam by a sudden blast from the hills of Bashan. The conquests of Cæsar and Alexander, the decrees of the Roman senate, the founding of Athens and Rome and Alexandria were events of trifling importance in the world's history, compared with the work which Jesus was doing, when he taught the multitudes on the shore of the lake, and called Simon, and Andrew, and James, and John, to forsake their nets and follow him.

These unlettered peasants of Galilee shall fulfill their divine commission with a wisdom and energy correspondent to its greatness. They shall acquire an unrivalled mastery over the cultivated mind of the world. They shall be quoted as supreme authority at the head of armies and in the councils of nations. They shall start revolutions in opinion before which the mighty fabric of old superstitions shall be cast down, and the profound theories of philosophers shall be changed to fables. They shall be more honored, and their lives and instructions shall be studied more earnestly, the higher the world rises in intellectual and moral cultivation. And all these mighty results shall flow from words which Jesus speaks to a company of poor, tired, hungry, disappointed fishermen, on the shore of the sea of Galilee. So truly was it one of the great hours of destiny for the world, when Jesus said to those wondering and awe-struck men, " Follow me."

We have only to listen to the words of Jesus as he speaks by the sea-side, and we shall be able to clothe the most striking features of the scene with living reality. Before him, in full sight, as he looks toward the people on the shore, is the fertile and beautiful plain of Gennesaret. The unfenced fields are divided only by foot-paths and land-marks. At this season of the year, in the tropical climate on the depressed level around the lake, the sower and the reaper may be seen scattering and gathering different kinds of grain side by side. On the slopes of the hills beyond, are shelving rocks, where the thin earth, moistened by the early rain, catches the first warmth of spring and shoots up the most rapid growth. When the rains cease and the sun shines all day from a cloudless sky, the premature growth withers away because it has no deepness of earth. Everywhere along the pathways in the neglected corners of the fields and up the hill-sides, may be seen tufts of thorns growing so thickly as to choke all other vegetation. The birds of the air are sporting and foraging for their morning meal in every direction, caring little for the cries of watchmen who are set upon towers and under booths to fray them away. There are no solitary farmhouses scattered through the cultivated lands. The sower, the reaper, the vintager, must all "go forth" from the town to their daily task.

All this can be seen by the multitude from the lake-side in the clear light of the morning, when Jesus takes up his parable and says, "A sower went forth to sow." The birds alighting upon the paths through the unfenced fields where some of the sower's seed would always fall, the thin earth of the stony places, already parched and withered by the advancing season, the stubborn thorns choking all useful vegetation, and the good ground bringing forth a hundred fold for the reaper's hand, are all in sight while the divine Teacher employs these natural similitudes in setting forth the reception of his word in the human heart. And he so binds up the great truths of the heavenly kingdom with these earthly things, that the sun and the rain, the seasons and the harvests, will continue to repeat his sacred lessons to the susceptible heart, so long as the world shall stand.

Alas! how many hearts are still like the hard-beaten track of the barren and dusty road, insensible as the pavement of the trodden street, open for the passage of all the world's burdens and business, but receiving the precious seed of the divine word only to have it stolen away by the first plunderer or tempter that passes. How many are like the thin earth upon the rock, receiving the message of life with sudden joy, burning with zeal to proclaim the new hope, rebuking the thoughtful and the considerate for coldness and delay, and yet all withered and lifeless under the increasing heat of trial and temptation, which is sent to bring forth fruit unto perfection. How many are like the neglected borders and corners of the field, so overgrown with thorny cares and anxieties, with earthly pleasures and ambitions, that the things of the heavenly kingdom can find no place in their hearts. And yet when the seed of the divine word falls into the good ground of an honest and believing heart, it is sure to bring forth fruit unto eternal life. Not only a hundred, but infinite fold shall be the harvest of peace and joy springing from a faithful reception of Christ's word by a single soul.

The whole western shore of the lake is gilded over with the yellow blossoms of a plant that grows by cultivation in the gardens, springs up unbidden among the wheat and barley, lines the pathways among the hills, and sheds its pungent fragrance on the air, at this season of the year, through the whole of Galilee. It is the wild mustard, growing so high above all kinds of grass and grain as to be called a tree. Birds alight upon its branches and laborers rest beneath its shadow. It springs from a seed so small as to afford a comparison for the least of anything; and it grows with irrepressible vitality all over the land.

All this is before the eye and familiar to the observation of all who listen when Jesus says, "The kingdom of heaven is like to a grain of mustard seed." In such vivid forms does he lodge in their wondering minds the germ of the great truth that the work begun by him in so simple a manner on the shore of that quiet lake, shall live and expand until it fills the earth. This little, fiery, pungent seed, which gives forth its power the more it is bruised, and which grows on every hill-side and in every valley in spite of all efforts to destroy it, shall help these poor Galileans to understand the quickening power, and the invulnerable life of the truth, which is to spread from the lips of Jesus over all lands and through all ages.

This wondrous kingdom of God, whose Prince appears as a Galilean peasant, who makes prime ministers of the poor, and takes a fishing boat for a throne, shall grow in greatness and in glory, until all the kingdoms of the earth become subject to its power, and all the principalities of heaven rejoice in its triumph. This promised unity of nations, which the princes and philosophers of this world could never comprehend; this mighty moral revolution, which is to make all other changes and conflicts the instruments of its own accomplishment, is the great germinal truth, planted by Jesus himself on the shores of the sea of Galilee, when teaching the multitude from a fishing boat. The fruit of that seed has already given life to millions, and it is destined to fill the earth with the abundance of peace and salvation.

This whole region has been repeatedly overrun and devastated by invading armies, and by roving bands of lawless men, whose sole object is to plunder and destroy. From the days of Solomon, and Joshua, and Abraham, the whole country around the lake has been subject to every change and calamity which can make life and property insecure. Princes have robbed peasants and merchantmen; government has robbed princes; conquerors have robbed all alike. Changes in the ruling power have been frequent and liable to occur at any time; and whatever the change, the holders of property must always suffer. For centuries it has been the study of the people to save property from robbery, extortion and conscription. It has become a maxim of prudence and foresight with the rich, that a third of one's possessions should be hidden in the earth.

This has been the feeling and the custom of the country for more than a thousand years. In many cases, the place of concealment has been forgotten or lost through the sudden death, imprisonment or exile of the only one who knew the secret. And so the impression is everywhere diffused, that immense sums may lie buried in any man's field or garden, and no living owner to claim them. Every one has heard tales of great riches suddenly acquired by the discovery of treasures hidden in the earth. Treasure-seeking has been taken up as a profession to the neglect of the regular pursuits of industry. Some go about the country, pretending to the art of detecting the place where money has been concealed. Men have fainted or become frantic with excitement upon discovering a trifling sum. The peasant in the fields, the householder in his garden, the traveler by the wayside, is all alive to any indication, that possibly he may light upon great riches hidden in the earth. All over Galilee men can be easily found, in any number, to dig all night in desperate earnestness and with the utmost secrecy, with the bare hope that some idle tale or mischievous invention of professional treasure-detectors may prove true.

Jesus speaks to men upon whose fervid imaginations all these wild traditions and extravagant expectations have taken effect from the earliest youth. In the midst of a country, where these customs have been universal for a thousand years, he draws the attention of the multitude to the only permanent and satisfying possession by saying, "The kingdom of heaven is like unto treasure hid in a field, the which, when a man hath found, he hideth, and for joy thereof goeth and selleth all that he hath and buyeth that field."

He would show them that there is an infinite treasure hidden where all who seek can find it. He has come to lead and direct the search.

The poorest who keep his word shall be made richer than all the princes of the earth. This infinite treasure can be found by every one, in the path where he walks, in the house where he lives. When found, it can be kept so as never to be lost, and he who possesses it, shall only be made richer by sharing it with others. To possess such a treasure, one can well afford to sell or sacrifice all else that he has.

2. THE SYNAGOGUE.

The Jews of Capernaum were proud of their synagogue. It was built by a Roman Centurion as a tribute of respect for their simple form of worship, and for the sublime truths of their religion. It was made of white marble, beautiful in proportions, and shining like the snows of Hermon in the morning sun. Its dazzling whiteness was the more conspicuous from contrast with the houses of black, volcanic rock with which it was surrounded. It was equal in dimensions to the temple of Solomon. Its colonnade and portico were of Grecian style, and the ruins of to-day remind the traveler of the fluted shafts and finished capitals of Ephesus and Athens. It stood upon the high ground, with its pillared front and lofty steps, wide as the whole structure, facing to the north. The whole upper portion of the building, ornamented with deeply carved flutings and flowers and acanthus leaves, rose above the surrounding houses of the city, and could be clearly seen from every town and village on the shore of the lake.

The worshipper dipped his hands in the water of a running fountain as he mounted the lofty steps. Then he reverently and solemnly crossed the marble floor of the broad portico, pushed aside the heavy curtain from the doorway, entered and bowed himself in prayer with his face towards Jerusalem. Once within the walls, he must leave all worldly employments and conversation without. The building itself, once dedicated to religious worship, must never be used for any other purpose.

At the upper end stood the ark or chest, in which the book of the law was kept; and the presence of the sacred scroll made that part of the building the most holy place. The lid of the chest was called the mercy seat, and a veil hung before it lest its sanctity should be profaned by too frequent exposure to vulgar eyes. Before the ark stood a golden candle-stick with eight branches, lighted only on great festivals, and a single silver lamp which was kept burning day and night. At this upper end of the synagogue were the "chief seats," which the scribes and Pharisees loved. In the central portion of the building, was a raised platform with a pulpit or reading desk in the middle. The minister of the congregation ascended the pulpit and the elders took their places upon the platform around him. The rich and titled personages vied with each other in securing the places of honor at the upper end. The common people came in like their superiors, bowing to the ark, and taking their places upon the wooden benches or the marble floor.

The ordinary service of the synagogue was a modification of the more stately and imposing service of the temple at Jerusalem. And the general form of service in Christian churches is a modification of the service of the synagogue. First was the prayer of invocation and praise. Then the whole congregation, led by ten men appointed to conduct the service of song, joined in singing the psalms of David. Then a person called the chazzan, who had the general care of the building, went up to the ark, reverently drew aside the veil, lifted the lid, took out the sacred scroll, carried it down to the chief elder, who was standing in the pulpit to read. An exposition or practical address followed the reading, and the scroll was carried back and replaced in the ark. As it was borne through the assembly, all followed it with their eyes, many rushed forward to touch and to press the sacred writing to their lips. Women stretched forward their hands weeping and the whole congregation manifested the deepest emotion. Prayer followed the reading of the scriptures and the address, and the congregation responded "Amen," to the petitions and benedictions of the elders.

When this formal service was completed, opportunity was given to any in the synagogue to speak. At the time when Jesus was going to and fro among the towns and cities of Galilee, it was a question constantly discussed in all religious assemblies, "when would the Messiah appear, and what would be the signs of his coming?" Jesus availed himself of this expectation and of the free speech accorded to all in the Sabbath service, to preach the gospel of the kingdom in all their synagogues. With this object in view, he often entered the beautiful marble temple which the Roman centurion had built for the Jews of Capernaum.

On one occasion when Jesus was there, the silence and decorum of the sacred place were rudely broken by the startling outcry of a wretched creature whom the demons of darkness had subjected to their cruel power. The holy presence of the divine Healer awakened the most passionate and contradictory emotions in the mind of the one possessed. The mighty woe which had been brought into his soul by the power of Satan, broke forth in a cry which seemed to come equally from the man himself, and from the evil one that tormented him. There still remained in the enslaved and darkened soul, light enough to disclose his own misery. The possessing demon felt and acknowledged the presence of the supreme Lord.

And yet the unhappy man wanted the power to make an earnest and consistent appeal to Jesus for help. When his enfeebled will strove to offer the prayer, the indwelling demon possessed his voice and made him utter the petition that Jesus would "let him alone." He was like one in a dream, feeling himself to be impelled towards the brink of some awful precipice, or about to be torn in pieces by wild beasts, all the while conscious that it is a dream, yet wanting the power to cry out or to shake off the spell which binds him. The will of the man was possessed by another and a cruel power, and yet he had freedom enough left to groan beneath the weight of the bondage which was upon him, and to desire deliverance by a mightier hand than his own. He had indeed first offered himself a prey to the powers of darkness by his own voluntary sin. He had opened the gate through which the enemy came in with his own hand, and so his captivity had begun. And yet he was not fully willing to give up the palace of the soul to the evil possession. And his yearning for redemption, though expressed by rude outcries and contradictions, brought him within reach of healing power.

The calm presence of Jesus awoke the tempest of fear and hope and renewed torment in his soul, just because he had not yet fully consented to be at peace with the Satanic tyranny which had crushed his manhood and bound debasing fetters upon his soul. The usurping demon put forth all his might to retain possession of the man, just because the divine Deliverer was there, and nothing better suits the malice of the powers of darkness than to hold their victim in the presence of the Prince of light. The wretched creature was torn and convulsed by the terrible struggle, and he gave utterance to his agony in groans and frantic outcries before all the assembly.

And how shall this conflict end? Only in one way; for by the confession of the demons themselves "the Holy One of God" was there, and the mightiest of their legions must obey his word. The evil spirit could only rend his victim with one last and terrible torture while leaving him; just as now, Satan is most active to tempt and torment the souls of those who are renouncing his power and dominion forever.

The time of our Lord's ministry would seem to have been the crisis of the great conflict between light and darkness in this world. The evil powers which had ruled with supreme dominion over men thus far, were summoned to meet their divine Antagonist with all their legions. And hence the demons were brought face to face with Jesus in the sanctuary, in private homes and in the desert. Their numbers were counted by single possessions, by sevens, and by legions. In this particular case, the defiant power followed Jesus into the synagogue on the Sabbath, and cried out with noisy and profane vehemence in the midst of the solemnities of divine worship and instruction.

Jesus silenced and cast out the foul spirit with a word. The soul of the one possessed, torn and tortured by one final paroxysm of the outgoing demon, was at last calm and free, in the presence of Jesus. The assembly in the synagogue, rightly counted this the most astonishing evidence, that Jesus was in very deed, the Holy One of God. They had never before seen or heard of one, who could command the unclean spirits with such authority, that they should silently and immediately obey him. By this single act, Jesus asserted and proclaimed his own complete mastery over the worst and over all the evils that have ever plagued and tortured the human race in all ages.

And here in this synagogue of Capernaum, on a quiet Sabbath morning, in the fullness of the Syrian spring, the power of the prince of darkness is for the first time crushed and put to shame. The great enemy which has deceived the nations for ages, and filled the earth with sin and misery, is smitten and dismayed by a single word from the lips of the Son of God. All other helps and healings, which men need for body or for soul, will be easily secured, when once the author of evil is overcome. He who gains the victory over the greatest foe, may well be trusted to do for us exceeding abundantly above all that we can ask or think. So the assembly in the synagogue of Capernaum understood the mighty work of Jesus, in silencing and dismissing the foul spirit that disturbed the morning service. For no sooner had the sun set, and the Sabbath ended, than all the city were gathered together at the door of the house where Jesus was. The lame, the sick, the paralytic, the possessed, were all there. Leaning upon the arm of friends, supported by crutches, carried in beds, they all came, with the full expectation that life and health would be theirs again, if only they could have access to him, whose single word had silenced and cast out the foul spirit in the synagogue that Sabbath morning. And they were not disappointed. Jesus healed them all. When the wretched and suffering, who crowded the street at sunset, went to their homes, they walked without help from friends. That night in Capernaum, sleep came to many a couch where quiet rest had long been a stranger. The next day, there was nothing for the physician to do in that city.

And a deeper peace, a more profound and blessed rest, would come to the hearts of millions, if only they could be persuaded to seek it from him, whose touch was life and health to the afflicted in the streets of Capernaum. He did all his mighty works of healing upon the

body, that he might prove his power and willingness to do a greater work upon the stricken and suffering soul. And into the streets of every city, into every house where the story of his life is read, he comes to do that greater work for all who need.

On another Sabbath morning, the presence of Jesus excited extraordinary interest in the synagogue of Capernaum. The night previous had been one of tempest and darkness on the lake. The storm raged with great violence from sunset to three o'clock in the morning, and then subsided with strange suddenness into a perfect calm, as the flame of a candle is blown out with a single breath. The waves, which ordinarily required many hours to become composed, after such agitation, ceased in the midst of their wildest commotion. One moment the lake was lifting itself up with convulsive billows, and groaning beneath the scourge of the winds; the next, it was smooth as a sea of glass.

The Sabbath morning was calm and bright, as if no tempest had ever shaken the earth or the sea. The assembly gathered in greater numbers than usual, and as they ascended the marble steps, and crossed the broad portico, there were signs of excitement and curiosity upon every face. The sudden cessation of the storm, the news that Jesus was already in the synagogue, when it was generally understood that the night left him on the opposite shore, the still stranger story told by some who came around on foot from Bethsaida before the Sabbath evening began, the startling rumor that the mass of the people were about to rise and set up Jesus for their king,—all this was quite enough to quicken the quiet step, and disturb the grave deportment, with which the assembly usually gathered for morning worship in the synagogue.

And besides the wonder and excitement only increased, when they learned more fully what had taken place the day before on the other side, and how the night had been spent by some on the lake. It was generally understood in Capernaum the day before, that Jesus had gone over with his disciples to the desert country on the eastern side of the lake. As the boat was seen to put off in that direction, and many knew that Jesus was on board, the people gathered in great numbers and ran afoot along the western shore and across the bridge of the Jordan at the upper end of the lake, and some were already waiting for him on the other side, when he came to the land. Not to be wholly deprived of the object for which he had withdrawn from Capernaum, he endeavored to steal away from the crowd, and secure a little retirement with his disciples.

But he was moved with compassion for the multitude, as they continued to gather, on foot and in boats from all the neighboring towns, and they seemed to him "as sheep having no shepherd." The crowd of people was greatly increased by additions from the annual caravan of pilgrims on their way to Jerusalem, to attend the great national feast of the passover.

Jesus came forth from his retreat, resolved to teach and to heal the sick, while the day lasted, and then to seek the retirement for which he longed, in the solitude and darkness of the night, on the mountains. Taking his seat upon the grassy hill-side, where he could be seen and heard by the vast assemblage, he continued to speak unto them, and to heal the sick that were brought to him, until the sun began to sink behind the hills of Galilee. And

then to save the thousands of weary, hungry, homeless people from perishing with faintness and fatigue, as they sought shelter for the night, Jesus fed all in the desert, with such simple food as they were accustomed to, and what remained of the feast, when all were filled, was more than the five loaves with which they began.

The astonished multitude cried, that he who could do such wonderful works, must indeed be the Messiah, and they were ready to seize on him by force, and carry him back in triumph to Capernaum for their king, when suddenly he disappeared from among them, and could no where be found.

Left to themselves, they were obliged to hurry back the way they came. For the Sabbath would begin at sunset, and the strictness with which they interpreted the law would forbid them to travel the distance of a mile, even for food or shelter, on the holy day. If the day closed upon them in that desert place, they would have to remain there till the next sunset, or else, in their estimate, break the commandment by traveling on the Sabbath. Gerasa, Bethsaida, Chorazin, Capernaum, Magdala, Tiberias, could all be reached in time by land or water, by those who started at the hour of the evening sacrifice. So all left the scene of the mighty miracle before sunset, the disciples themselves being constrained by Jesus to take to their boat and leave him in the desert place alone.

All this was known to the assembly, gathering in the synagogue of Capernaum the next morning. But many who came around to the city by land the previous evening, were surprised to find Jesus himself at his usual place among the worshippers. Then the disciples increased their surprise by telling the story of the night on the lake; the fury of the storm; the nine hours of hard rowing against the wind; the appearance of Jesus walking upon the sea; the cry of alarm, and then the impulsive attempt of Peter to go out to meet him on the water; the rescue of the sinking disciple; the hushing of the storm, and the subsidence of the waves, the moment that Jesus came on board; the safe return of all to the Gennesaret shore, and the purpose already formed to send messengers, as soon as the Sabbath sun was set, all over Galilee to bring in the sick and afflicted to be healed.

All this was quite enough to fill the minds

of the assembly in the synagogue with wonder and curiosity to know the meaning of what they had heard. They could scarcely wait for the ordinary service to close before they gathered about Jesus, and began to question him with great eagerness and severity.

"How came he there so early in the morning, when the evening left him on the other side of the lake? Could he repeat the miracle of the previous day, and support all his followers, as the fathers were fed with bread from heaven in the wilderness? Had he in very deed walked upon the sea and hushed the storm? And could he give health, and strength, and riches, and long life to all who would set him up for a prince in the land? What new and great sign could he show them of his authority to restore the nation and redeem Israel?"

To all such questions, Jesus only replied by exposing their worldly and selfish motives in seeking him, and by declaring that he himself was the bread of life. The manna of Moses and the bread of yesterday's miracle, could only appease hunger and sustain life for a time.

Believing in him, they should never die. His own flesh and blood must be given in sacrifice for the world, and they must live by faith in that sacrifice, or there could be no life in them. He had indeed healed the sick, and fed the hungry, and raised the dead. He had hushed the winds, and walked upon the waves. But he had not come to change the order of nature, to bestow health without sickness, or harvests without labor. It was not his great work to bring in a material millennium of national aggrandizement and earthly prosperity. It was his great office to give eternal life, and possessing that, they need give themselves little anxiety about things that perish.

The gross minds and dark hearts of the Galileans could make little of such sayings, and that single discourse of Jesus in the synagogue, dissipated all the enthusiasm of the multitude to array themselves under such a leader. If their grand distinction as his followers must be a spiritual and a holy life, they would rather look for another Messiah.

And alas! for the scattered tribes of Israel, that, to this day, they should look only for a

Deliverer, who shall give the meat that perisheth, and not that which endureth unto eternal life. And alas! for the millions of every race lost in sin and misery, that they too should be ready to compass sea and land for some trifling earthly good, and yet turn away from Him who alone has the words of eternal life. Like blinded Israel, the world still waits for a Messiah, who shall give kingdoms and crowns, riches and glory, life and happiness on the earth. Whoever promises to relieve bodily suffering, to open new sources of wealth, to multiply the means of present enjoyment without imposing the task of personal reformation, will have hearers and followers without number. But he who offers infinite riches, eternal blessedness as the consequence and the reward of a holy life, a life of duty, of benevolence and self-denial, may have to mourn that his most earnest pleading and his most faithful instruction seem to others like an idle tale.

Science labors to explain all the mysteries of nature, of providence and of man's immortal being without one word of homage to Christ, without any reference to the need or the reality of redemption. The highest conceptions of art, the most delicate refinements of taste, often spring from utterly sensual and earthly minds. Literature is ever adding to its already exhaustless resources of wit and argument and passion and invention, all fitted and designed to persuade men to live for this world alone.

And so too the necessities of labor, the seductions of pleasure, the responsibilities of public life, the pressure of business, the demands of society are all assigned as helps or excuses or temptations, by reason of which men easily forget the infinite necessity of the soul, the infinite inheritance of glory and immortality. Christ alone has the words of eternal life. The dark problems of duty and of destiny become clear only when studied in the light which shines from the cross. The life of the poorest and lowliest man on earth becomes great and infinitely precious to him when once he learns to receive and improve it as a redeemed and everlasting possession for the Son of God.

3. THE MOUNT.

Let us now leave the narrow streets and the stone synagogue, the white beach and the fishing boats of Capernaum, and fall into one of

LAKE OF GALILEE.

the many dark lines of early travelers, who are climbing the winding foot-paths toward the mount of the Beatitudes just above the city. Having accomplished the ascent, and taken our seat with the multitude upon the grassy slope of the mount, let us listen to the gracious words of the divine Teacher, and observe what allusions he makes to objects around him.

It is the morning hour. Jesus had spent the night in solitude on the mountain. His withdrawal in that direction had been observed at evening, and the multitude have come up from the city and the villages by the lake-side in search of him at this early hour. Seeing them approach in great numbers, he comes part-way down the height to a level place to meet them. The sun is climbing the eastern heavens, and the surface of the lake shines like a sea of fire between the dark walls of its encompassing shores: Far away to the north, the snowy height of Hermon rises like a cloud of incense offered by the eternal hills in morning worship to the King of heaven. The surrounding heights and valleys, with all their varied outlines of barren cliffs, and green terraces, and wild ravines, stand forth to view with startling clearness in the blaze of light. The suddenness with which the dawn gives place to the day and wakes the sleeping world, makes it seem as if the risen sun were the infinite source of life and blessing to all creatures that live. The flowers put on a new beauty, the foliage wears a deeper green, the birds sing with a chorus of gladness, the flocks go forth with joy to their mountain pasturage at the return of the light.

Jesus, first addressing the little company of his disciples, who are to preach his gospel to all nations, says, "Ye are the light of the world." Great as is the change when the shades of night disappear, and the morning pours its glories on the hills of Galilee, it shall be a greater transformation when the night of ignorance and superstition passes away, and the nations wake to hear the voice of the Son of God. The sun goes forth in the heavens to fill the world with light. In like manner the disciples of Jesus shall go into all the dark places of the earth and make the truth shine around their path until the waste blooms with the beauty of paradise restored.

The surrounding hills are crowned with villages, whose white houses gleam with dazzling brightness in the morning sun. No true picture of the landscape would fail to make these shining mountain cities most conspicuous and attractive to every eye. And Jesus takes up his parable from them, and says, "A city set on a hill cannot be hid." The life and homes and instructions of those that follow him shall be the light and landmarks of all future history until the Lord's house is exalted among the hills, and all nations flow unto it.

Winding through the green fields, and climbing up the terraced hill-sides may be seen narrow paths, white and shining with the earthy residuum of salt which has lost its savor, and has been cast forth upon the barren walk to be trodden under foot of men. In the utter rejection of the worthless substance, Jesus shows the doom of those who prove false to their high commission, to keep his truth and to save the perishing.

The distant hills of Bashan are in sight beyond the lake. They have been the haunt of robbers and outlaws for ages. The listening multitudes have heard many tales of murder and crime committed by the dwellers in that wild region, and they suppose that to such men, no pity can be due in this world, and nothing can be in reserve for them, but the fires of gehenna, in the world to come. Rude, violent and denunciatory in speech, and accustomed to cursing even when talking with friends, yet commending themselves for their freedom from great crimes of violence, they shudder and look at each other with wonder when they hear the words of Jesus, "Whosoever shall say, thou fool, shall be in danger of the gehenna fire."

Pleasure boats are darting out from Tiberias and Magdala for a morning sail on the lake; and it is usual for the officers of Herod's government and the Roman army, to be there with their guilty paramours, leading lives of lust and dissipation, and the crowds from the streets of Capernaum are waiting to hear the holy Prophet of Nazareth pour out his denunciations upon these foreigners and imitators of foreign manners, who are accounted sinners above all them that dwell in Galilee. But they blush and hang their heads for shame when they hear him declare that the guilt of the outward life is in the secret thought of the heart. They are constrained to confess that in themselves they may secretly cherish the fruitful source of all that appears so shameless and revolting in the greatest criminals.

While he is speaking, trumpets sound the reveille for the Roman troops garrisoned in the cities on the lake shore. The long-drawn note rings out upon the clear silent air, and dies away in prolonged echoes among the hills. At the signal, soldiers can be seen coming forth for their morning parade upon the narrow plain below. As they take their places in the ranks they bow in military homage to the golden eagle, which the Jews look upon as the hated and idolatrous sign of subjection to a foreign power. The turbulent Galileans can never see that standard lifted up with the customary salutation of trumpets and voices, without feelings of bitterest hatred and revenge. And now the listening throng are impatient to hear what words of wrath the war note of the heathen power will bring forth from the lips of this promised Deliverer of Israel. But what does he say to inflame the passions of his hearers against the idolatrous and oppressive conquerors? "I say unto you love your enemies, bless them that curse you, do good to them that hate you, and pray for them that despitefully use you and persecute you."

A Roman courier, with half a dozen soldiers, comes up the high bank from the lake, making his way across the hills westward, as a bearer of despatches to Sephoris, the capital of Galilee, and thence to Rome. As he passes in sight of the great assembly, he falls in with peasants who are going out, in the early morning, to work in their fields and vineyards. The soldiers compel the poor laborers to go along with them and carry their arms and baggage up the steep ascent of the mountain road. It is a common act of oppression, and it is often accompanied with brutal provocations and blows. But while the multitudes are looking on with indignation, and a burning desire to revenge the wrong, the voice of the divine Teacher again arrests their attention. "I say unto you that ye resist not evil, but whosoever shall smite thee on the right cheek, turn to him the other also, and whosoever shall compel thee to go a mile, go with him twain."

It is now midsummer, and the work of sow-ing and reaping is going on at the same time, in the fertile plain of Gennesaret, where the fields are green and flowers blossom every month of the year. The tillers of the soil are busily gathering what has already grown, and anxiously watching that which is still immature, hoping and fearing, as husbandmen always do. Fishermen who draw their living from the lake, are watching the signs of wind and rain, and waiting for favorable nights to fill their nets. And so, in one direction and another, on the land and the lake, in the towns and the fields, the shepherd and the vintager, the merchant and the artisan, are anxiously pursuing their daily tasks, and dreading the consequences, should their labors prove unsuccessful.

At the same time, flocks of birds, sporting on the wing and in the water, make the morning air musical with their happy voices, and beat the waves into foam with their fluttering wings The joyous creatures attract the attention of the multitudes only to awaken the fear that the harvest will be devoured in the fields, and the fish on the shore will be frightened beyond the reach of their nets. And then the calm voice of Jesus takes up the fear and leads it on to faith,—"Why take ye thought, why are ye anxious about food, or raiment, or life? Behold the fowls of the air. For they sow not, neither do they reap, nor gather into barns; yet your heavenly Father feedeth them. Are ye not much better than they?"

The listening multitude are mostly poor. They have scarce clothing enough for comfort or decency, and they wear the same coarse garment through all the year. A rough mantle of camel's hair thrown across the shoulders and bound around the body with a leathern girdle is all that peasants and fishermen can boast for ornament or for use. In summer and in winter, in the houses and in the fields, by night and by day, they wrap themselves in the same soiled and shaggy covering. They have sat down, by hundreds and by thousands, on the grassy hill-sides to listen, desiring nothing so much as that the miraculous power of the new Prophet will be put forth in clothing them like princes, and enriching them with the spoil of their heathen conquerors.

The dark throng contrasts strangely with the bright hues of flowers that bloom everywhere in sight, from the lake-side, through the green valleys and oak woods, upward to the base of Tabor and over the hills towards Nazareth. And again the voice of the wondrous speaker foreruns the wish of all who hear, "And why take ye thought for raiment? Consider the lilies of the field how they grow; they toil not, neither do they spin: and yet I say unto you that even Solomon in all his glory was not arrayed like one of these."

The whole region in which Jesus is teaching has been many times overrun by devastating armies. The Babylonian, the Persian, the Syrian, the Greek and the Roman, have all passed that way, foraging in the fields and laying heavy exactions upon the towns. The open country has always been infested by wild beasts and robbers. For mutual safety the people are obliged to live in villages, strongholds and walled cities, the gates of which are guarded by day and shut by night. In many directions from the mount of the Beatitudes, the people can see the way of approach to the hill towns, climbing up the steep, winding along the precipice, terminating at the guarded gate. Whoever would rest in peace, must be found within the walls when the sun goes down. The people are weary of this continual watching against danger. They long for the time when all cities can keep open and unguarded gates, day and night, and the tired wayfarer can find admission without asking and at any hour; and the peasant can repose in safety under his own vine and fig-tree in the field, without seeking the protection of the town at all. And from this universal desire to be released from the necessity of effort and watching, Jesus takes up his parable and declares that entrance to the city that hath everlasting foundations, must be sought in time and with agonizing effort, or it will never be found. "Strive to enter in at the strait gate, for many, I say unto you, will seek to enter in, and shall not be able when once the Master hath shut to the door."

The multitude, gathered upon the mountain-side above Capernaum, to hear the words of Jesus had come from Galilee and from Decapolis, and from Jerusalem, and from Judæa, and from beyond Jordan. Some of them had lived in reed and mud-built hovels which a gust of wind would blow away or a dash of rain would level with the earth. Some had lived in houses the foundations of which rested upon a rock, and the walls of which had been standing for more than a thousand years and are standing to this day. Some lived in narrow valleys, the bed of which was sometimes dry and sometimes filled with a rushing and roaring torrent, that swept everything but the solid rock before it. Across the lake could be seen wild ravines and gorges, down which the cold winds of Hermon and Bashan swept with a fury that prostrated everything in its way, and ploughed up the sea into a phrensy of foam. Many had looked forth from their safe habitations on the high places of the rock, while the swollen streams rushed below, and descending torrents of rain filled all the air. Many had seen the place where the indolent and thoughtless man had built his house, and lived for a few seasons upon the pleasant and more accessible plain, and then at last, when the winter storms broke with unusual violence upon the hills, was himself swept away by the swollen torrent with the ruin of his own dwelling.

Surely such an audience would feel the force of the warning in the promise with which Jesus concludes his sermon on the mount, "Whoso heareth and doeth these sayings of mine, shall be like the wise, who build on the rock. And whoso heareth these sayings of mine and doeth them not shall be like the foolish, who build on the sand."

For eighteen hundred years, faith has kept the sayings of Jesus, and built upon himself as the living Rock. The storms of persecution and the floods of sorrow, and the strong winds of calamity, have blown and beaten upon that structure, but it still stands, for it is founded upon the eternal Rock. For eighteen hundred years, unbelief has been building upon the shifting sands of human opinion, and worldly interest, and proud speculation, and nothing built upon that foundation has been able to stand. Amid all the tempests that have swept the earth, the firm house, the impregnable fortress, the holy temple of our Christian faith, has stood secure upon its high and eternal Rock. Though veiled at times in clouds, it has come forth brighter from the darkness of every storm. The floods which have carried away its outer defenses of human forms, have only shown more clearly the firmness of its true foundation. And this stronghold of faith, which rests upon Christ, as the living and eternal Rock, shall remain secure, offering rest to the weary, and a hiding-place to the perishing, till the last tempest breaks.

BETHESDA.

Now there is at Jerusalem a pool called Bethesda, and a certain man was there, which had an infirmity thirty and eight years. When Jesus saw him lie, and knew that he had been now a long time in that case, he saith unto him, Wilt thou be made whole?—JOHN v. 2, 5, 6.

IV.

BETHESDA.

BETHESDA, house of mercy, a name of promise, and a promise wondrously fulfilled on the day when Jesus came there with His power to heal, and His mercy to forgive.

His Gospel makes the world a house of mercy to all that hear the joyful sound. We boast of justice in our dealings with our fellowmen; but there is nothing of which we have so much reason to be afraid, as that God shall treat us as we deserve. Justice alone, untempered with mercy, would make the world a prison-house for the guilty. It would thunder from the heavens with voices of vengeance. It would flame from the earth with fires of wrath. It would poison the air with pestilence. It would make every human habitation a house of mourning. It would send the thrill of pain through every fibre of the human frame. It would answer every desire of the heart with disappointment. It would make life a burden, and death the beginning of endless despair. Such would be the consequence to us all, were God to answer the prayer of the proud heart —"Give me only that which is my own. Let the justice of my claim be the measure of thy bounty."

But Jesus the Redeemer comes into a world which sin has made one great lazar-house of diseased and suffering humanity, and His presence makes it a house of mercy to millions. Mercy shines in the morning light, and mercy gilds the setting day. Mercy sings in the laughing stream, and shouts in the darkening storm. Mercy tempers the summer's heat and the winter's cold; revives the parched earth with the blessed rain; clothes the landscape with beauty, and crowns the year with goodness. Mercy flies on the wings of angels to the support of the feeble; to the defense of the poor; to the pardon of the guilty. Mercy broods with bleeding heart over the bloody field where armies meet in mortal strife, and watches amid scenes of horror and agony when the glory and the magnificence of battle have rolled away. Mercy brings the message of hope to the despairing, of joy to the sorrowing, of rest to the weary, and of life to the dead. Mercy removes the sting of the last bitter hour, and pours the glory of Paradise upon the vision that is dim with the shadows of death. Mercy makes a house of God in every place where the penitent bow in prayer. Mercy gives immortal life to all who look to Jesus to be "made whole."

What a pitiable scene is presented by this house of mercy at Jerusalem, named Bethesda! The marble floors of its five colonnades are covered with a miserable multitude, whose silent aspect is a cry of woe, and whose bare presence in such a place is a confession of affliction and infirmity. The sick, the feeble, the blind, are all here for the same purpose, and hoping to receive help from the same source.

Here, two faithful sons have brought their poor paralyzed old father, and set him down with his feet in the edge of the pool, and they are watching eagerly at his side, ready to take him up and rush in at the first movement of the healing wave. Close by their side sits a mother, with anxiety and sorrow written in every line of her face, as she looks tenderly and caressingly upon the paler face of her infant child; and she is there hoping to secure the baptism of the agitated waters in behalf of her poor babe, that she may not be left to bear the burden and the woe of life's weary journey alone. There a young wife, with the hectic glow of consumption burning upon her wasted cheek, leans, panting for breath, upon her husband's strong arm, feeling that but for one earthly tie, it were better for her if the bitterness of death were already past. Here an aged mother is trying to persuade her affectionate daughter to lead her home, and let her lie down upon her bed and die in peace without seeking to prolong a life that has already had too many sorrows.

Here the blind have been led by friendly hands, and seated on the margin of the pool, with their sightless eye-balls seeking in vain for light in the noon-tide blaze of the sun.

Here the wretched paralytic lies helpless, with the half of himself already dead, and wishing that the other half would die too, or that both might live together. Here are some so withered, and old, and poor, that one would wonder what life could be worth to them, unless indeed the healing waters can give them back the days of their youth.

Some are attended by many friends, who cheer them with words of hope, and relieve their sufferings with every possible attention. Some have exhausted their utmost strength in dragging themselves to the house of mercy alone. Some are uttering cries of impatience and pain; some are sinking and fainting with exhaustion; some are waiting in calm and trustful silence for the rippling of the water when it shall be swept by the viewless angel's wing. The long colonnade is crowded through its whole extent, and the wants and woes of the human race are represented by the multitude drawn together by the mysterious power of that healing fountain.

Among the friends of the afflicted and the throng of idle spectators, a stranger enters the portico unobserved. He passes along with a quiet step and a pitying look, till his eye falls upon the most helpless and wretched of all the company. For thirty-eight years that miserable man has been bound to a crippled and suffering body, and the long and dreadful servitude has crushed his spirit and broken his heart. The lustre of life has faded from his eye, and the expression of interest from his face. His whole personal appearance is most wretched and revolting, and the rest of the company shrink from approaching or addressing him. He is shunned the more carefully for the reason that his infirmity is known to have been caused by his own sin, and he is looked upon as smitten of God, and accursed. He has no one to help him when the favored moment comes to enter the water. The troubled wave betrays the presence of a new life that never quickens him. For years he has spread his miserable mat upon the stone floor at the very edge of the pool, waiting for the all-healing angel to descend, but never has he been able to enter the troubled water in time to be made whole. And he has grown so old and impotent, and his long misery has so nearly crushed the life out of him, that many wonder why he need exhaust his little remaining strength in creeping down to his

old place, when his continual coming has done him no good. Many wish he would not come to shock the sensibilities of others with the sight of his wretchedness.

On him the quiet stranger looks with a pitying eye, till his attention is arrested, and then He puts the startling question, "Wilt thou be made whole?" Made whole! For what other purpose has he dragged his crippled frame to that healing fountain? For what else has he longed and groaned in spirit for thirty-eight years? What other blessing could he crave so earnestly, while the faintest gleam of hope continued to shine in his enfeebled and darkened mind? But now it seems almost like mockery to ask him the question, for there is no eye to pity, and no arm to help him. The healing movement of the waters is all for others, not for him.

But the wretched man has not half uttered his despondency, before the eye that is fixed upon him seems to kindle with a benignant and divine light. The countenance of the stranger assumes a most fascinating and commanding majesty which nothing can resist. The helpless creature already feels that he could travel to the ends of the earth at one word from such a face as that. And no sooner thought than uttered, the quickening and creative word comes, "Arise—walk."

There is no delay, no doubt, no question. The diseased and despondent listener feels new life rushing through every fibre of his frame. Hope flashes like a new heaven upon his darkened mind. He can, he will, he must obey that voice, and, in the act of obedience, he becomes at once the strongest and soundest man in the multitude. He, who it was thought would be the last to receive aid from the healing fountain, is the first to be made whole without its help.

The eyes of all are fixed upon him with astonishment as he springs to his feet, throws the matting on which he was lying across his arm, and walks forth with the firm and elastic step of youth. Excited spectators crowd around him; the colonnade is filled by additional numbers attracted from without; the sick forget to watch for the movement of the water; the Sabbath stillness that reigned through all the porticos a moment before is broken by the clamor of many voices; every one is asking who has done this mighty work; and, in the meantime, the mysterious stranger, whose word alone has made the man whole, disappears, and is nowhere found.

The world is one great lazar-house of diseased and suffering souls, and Jesus comes, in the message of his word, to make them whole. He comes to you, whose eye now falls upon this page, and his presence makes the place where you read a house of mercy. The first awakening call of the Gospel to every soul is still the same as that which fell from the lips of Jesus in the porches of Bethesda: "Wilt thou be made whole?" This is the great question of redemption in answer to the great cry of humanity—"Who will show us any good?" Christ comes as a Saviour, a Healer, a Redeemer, and the help which he offers is sufficient for the utmost sorrows and necessities of the human race.

It is not a partial or a temporary relief which he brings. He would make the wounded spirit whole. He would save from a death that shall never die. He looks upon us in love that we may see in his eye the promise of something better than the world can give.

And when kindness fails to arrest our attention, he tries the greater kindness of chastisement and sorrow. He sends afflictions and disappointments that are bitter to the soul, that he may awaken the sense of need, that he may call forth the imploring cry—"What shall I do to be saved?" That cry must be awakened at whatever cost, or the fatal lethargy of sin will go on until it deepens into complete and endless death.

The three great moral faculties of the soul are faith, hope and love, and these lie all paralyzed and inactive until Christ comes to give them life.

Faith is the living hand by which the soul takes hold on infinite help. Faith is the conducting medium by which the renewed heart is made to beat in unison with the heart of infinite love. Faith lifts the veil from the unseen world and displays the glories of the paradise above. Faith lightens the burden and relieves the weariness of life by anticipating the rest of heaven. Faith rejoices in the depths of affliction, conquers in the great fight of temptations, waxes stronger under every trial of its strength, reposes for protection under the overshadowing throne of the Most High.

And yet without Christ, there is no assured foundation on which such faith can rest. He alone is the Author and the Finisher of faith. He comes to the poor, the helpless and the guilty, saying, "Believe and thou shalt see the glory of God; believe and thou shalt be saved; believe and thou shalt never die."

Hope is the recovered treasure, the loss of which had left the soul utterly poor and undone. Hope can sustain the soul like a sure and tried anchor amid all the tempests and agitations of the world; it can give confidence and peace when the heavens are dark, and the journey of life is ending in the valley of the shadow of death.

Without Christ the soul is utterly without hope, and he comes upon the mission of mercy to bring back the lost treasure, and to make every soul who will receive him infinitely and forever rich in the possession of the hope of eternal life.

Love is the golden chain which binds the

believing soul in willing bonds to the service of the supreme Sovereign, to the society of the holy and the blessed, to the maintenance of justice and truth forever and ever. Love lifts the ransomed soul from the deeps of despair, and gives it wings to climb the highest heaven, and a voice to sing its great Redeemer's praise in sweeter strains than angels ever sung.

And Christ comes to quicken, in every soul that receives his word, the paralyzed capacity for such love, and to kindle the faintest spark of spiritual life into immortal flame. Christ comes to lift up the depraved and darkened slave of sin, and make him a fit companion for the seraph that adores in the highest heaven, and shines the brightest in the splendors of the eternal throne.

These three great moral faculties of man—faith, hope and love, without the use of which he is a paralyzed and helpless creature—this immortal triad of powers, by the exercise of which man enlists the help of Omnipotence, is all in ruins until Christ comes with the word of life. He comes to give soundness and unconquerable vitality to man's ruined nature by renewing its decayed and unused capacities for faith, hope and love.

To you who read these lines, Jesus comes pityingly as he came to the man in Bethesda. To you he speaks with a voice which blends so quietly with your own thought that it seems like the voice of your own heart. "Wouldst thou be made whole? Wouldst thou have every faculty of thy spiritual and immortal nature restored to a sound and healthful life? Wouldst thou be brought into such a state of intelligent and happy agreement with thyself as that the lessons of experience, the deductions of reason, the monitions of conscience, shall be always and willingly obeyed? Wouldst thou have thy whole moral being so completely renovated and glorified as that to thee all things shall become new; the world shall be full of beauty; the pathway of life shall be strewn with blessing; every loss shall be attended with greater gain; every disappointment shall be the promise of greater good; every affliction shall be crowned with mercy, and death shall come only to give the crown of life?"

All this would Jesus gladly do for every soul. It is not necessary for any one to give up his heart to be wasted with vain conflicts, to be consumed with unanswered desire. There is rest for the weary even here, and Christ will give it to all who ask him. Many times, in many forms, he puts the question: "Wilt thou be made whole?" When you felt yourself drawn to the book of God by a secret and gentle power, and a sudden light flashed upon the page as you read, and it seemed, for the moment, as if it had been all written for you; when the preaching of the Divine word and the ordinary service of the sanctuary made an unusually solemn and persuasive appeal to your heart; when the prayer that went up from human lips seemed, in very deed, to take hold on God, and to bring the awful realities of eternity near; then Christ was stirring, in your own heart, the startling question which he put to the man in Bethesda, "Wilt thou be made whole?"

When the failure of worldly plans, the disappointment of cherished hopes, the death of beloved friends, the near approach of the eternal world under the shadow of sickness or danger, made all earthly things seem vain and incapable of satisfying the supreme necessities of the soul, then Christ was drawing near and putting the question seriously, tenderly, to your heart: "Wilt thou be made whole?"

When the love of Christ seemed to put on a new and strange beauty and drew you to his cross with a resistless power, and conscience declared the sin of neglecting that power to be very great, and you could not repress the longing of your heart for a better portion than earth can give; then Christ was looking upon you with tenderness and pity, as he looked on the wretched man at Bethesda, saying: "Wilt thou be made whole?"

When some strange light revealed the hidden depth of sin in your own heart, and you were so alarmed and horror-struck by the discovery, that you were ready to cry out, "Oh! wretched man that I am! Who shall deliver me from the body of this death?" Then the Friend of the friendless, the Saviour of sinners, was saying to you with such compassion as he showed to the afflicted on earth: "Look unto Me and be saved. I have borne thine iniquities; by the stripes laid on me thou canst be healed."

So, in a thousand ways, is Christ ever urging upon every hearer of his Gospel the acceptance of the greatest possible blessing, a restored spiritual life, a sound, healthful and happy exercise of the best and noblest faculties of the soul. Everything which can make existence a blessing, everything for which the deathless soul was created, is staked upon obedience to the word of Christ, when he says: "Come unto me." The glory, the blessedness and the joy of an eternal life are his who looks to Christ and to him alone for help. The conditions upon which he bestows infinite riches are such as to bring the gift of life within the reach of the poorest and the worst.

We must come to Christ confessing our need. He comes to us as a Saviour, and we shall never receive him to our hearts until we feel that, without him, we are lost, utterly and forever. He comes to make us whole, to deliver us completely and forever from the dreadful disease of sin. To derive help from him, we must feel that to live in sin is death, and to die without a Saviour is endless despair. Our great need, our utterly lost and hopeless state must be our great argument in applying to an infinite Saviour for help. And we must be truthful and candid in confessing that we are lost in ourselves, and then we shall look the more earnestly to him for salvation.

We must go to Christ sincerely desiring such help as he is prepared to give. His name and his character, his life and his death fulfill the promise; "He shall save his people from their sins." Such a salvation we must seek in coming to Jesus with sincere hearts.

It is not simply rescue from punishment, it is a holy life, a life of faith, and love, and obedience to God, that we need. This is the healing which the word of Christ alone can give. And every sinner should be ready to say to Christ: "I come to thee for help, that I may get the mastery of my evil heart, that I may lead a holy life, that I may be made whole from this very hour. I ask no earthly gift. I am willing to toil, to wait, and to suffer all the days of my appointed time of trial and of duty, if, at last, I may be with thee, and find my name written in thy book of life."

We must look to Christ expecting to find help. We cannot trust him too much or too soon. We cannot over estimate his power or his willingness to grant us pardon, peace and salvation. He has died for our redemption, and what can he do more to convince us of his desire to save? Inquirers for the way of salvation wait and wonder that they are so long in finding the object of their search, because they do not expect to find it. They are not ready to take the hand which Christ offers them and walk with him, and therefore they are still wandering and in darkness. They are not yet fully resolved to take up the cross at once, trusting that strength will be given them to bear it, and therefore they are bearing the heavier burden of their own sins. We must look to Jesus as we look to a tried and faithful friend in time of need, confident that our necessities will touch his heart, and that we have only to make known our wants to be sure of his sympathy and support.

When Jesus entered the crowded porches of Bethesda, he sought out the most hopeless and wretched of all the impotent multitude, and made that helpless creature whole in a moment, that he might inspire all others with confidence in his power to save. We cannot trust such a Saviour too much, or too soon. To be forgiven, to have the dark record of our sins blotted out forever, to be made heirs of eternal life, we need no worth of our own; no human friend can help us; it is in vain to wait for stronger persuasions, or better opportunities, or holier dispositions. We must go to Christ, and to him alone. We must go to him just as we are, and with full confidence in his power to save. He has done all for us, just because we can do nothing for ourselves. He is rich enough to answer all our need. He is merciful enough to forgive all our sins. He desires of us nothing so much as that we shall be willing to take the crown of life from his own hands.

TABOR.

And it came to pass about an eight days after these sayings, he took Peter and John and James, and went up into a mountain to pray. And as he prayed, the fashion of his countenance was altered, and his raiment was white and glistering. And, behold, there talked with him two men, which were Moses and Elias: who appeared in glory, and spake of his decease which he should accomplish at Jerusalem.—LUKE ix. 28–31.

V.

TABOR.

THE earthly ministry of our Lord supplies three subjects of most profound and commanding interest, to all readers of the Gospels; the miracles, the parables, and the passion. His mighty works arrested attention. His divine instructions disclosed his true character and the object of his mission. His atoning death completed his work and confirmed the truthfulness of all he had spoken.

The mighty works would have been inexplicable without the divine word. The perfect life would have been a still greater mystery without the atoning death. Sight was given to the blind, that truth might find entrance to the soul. The cross was borne by the king, that his redeemed subjects might share his crown. This great mystery of suffering is what the disciples found it hardest to understand. The awful glory of the transfiguration was undoubtedly displayed to keep alive their feeble faith in him as the Messiah, when once he had begun to teach them that he must be rejected and crucified at Jerusalem.

He had extended his journeyings northward to the utmost boundaries of Palestine. Out of the reach of Herod and of Caiaphas, with nothing to fear from Jew or Roman, he takes this opportunity to make the terrible announcement to his devoted followers, that he must yet go back to Jerusalem and give himself up to die. His hour will come and no earthly hand can stay its approach. The sacrifice was appointed from the foundation of the world, and it must be fulfilled though heaven and earth should pass away. And, to make this declaration still more dark and afflicting to his disciples, it followed immediately upon the assurance that he was the Christ, the Son of the living God.

He had just told them, in the most solemn and explicit terms, that he would establish his kingdom in the earth so firmly that the gates of hell should not prevail against it. He had commended Peter for declaring his confidence in his divine character. He had said, that his Father in heaven had made that revelation to the believing disciple. He had claimed the crown and accepted the title of God's anointed Son. And now he says that he must go to Jerusalem, submit to shame and torture, and be put to death. Now he rebukes Peter with the utmost severity, for daring to hint that such a dreadful thing could not come to pass. After having excited their hopes to the highest pitch, he even goes on to tell them that they too must bear the cross and suffer shame, or they can never share his glory. His own suffering must be completed in them, and his crucifixion to the world must be perpetuated in the experience of his disciples for all time.

Six days intervened between the time of making these startling disclosures to his followers and the transfiguration. To them, the days were full of sadness and perplexity. They had many reasonings with themselves, as they journeyed southward from Cesarea Philippi beside the waters of Merom, and along the shores of the sea of Galilee, toward the fatal city, where ignominy and death awaited their Master. As they went on day after day from village to village, and from one province to another, it must have seemed passing strange to them, that he could go, voluntarily and unbidden, to meet the very doom which would be ruin to all their hopes, and grief to all their hearts.

They could not venture to remonstrate, or to dissuade him from his purpose; for he had already denounced all such interference as suggestions of Satan. They could not renounce all hope that he might yet prove himself to be the Son of the Highest, because he was daily putting forth his mighty power in such works as no mere man could do. Their minds were still dazzled and allured by the glory and riches which they hoped to enjoy with him in his earthly kingdom. And yet all the while he was leading them towards the scene of his rejection and shame, his crucifixion and death.

Six days are past by them in utter perplexity and sorrow. And now the time has come when the disciples must receive some additional testimony to the Messiahship of their beloved Master, or they will lose all faith in his divine mission; they will no longer look to him as the one to redeem Israel.

It is drawing towards evening. The laborers are gathering in from the vineyards and

the harvest fields, to the villages. The bleating flocks are returning to the folds on the grassy slopes of Tabor. The snowy heights of distant Hermon are reddening in the glow of the setting sun. Mount Carmel casts its lengthening shadows far up the plain of Esdraelon The deep silence which settles down upon the solitudes of nature, invites to retirement, meditation and prayer.

And now the Master calls the three favorite disciples to himself, and makes his way out of the noisy town, across the open fields and the wild pasture lands, and up the steep ascent of the mountain. It is a rounded and dome-like elevation, pushed up to a great height, out of the bosom of the plain. The evening cloud sweeps beneath the summit, and the light of the setting sun lingers long upon the top, after it has left the plain below.

The path first leads through waving fields of golden grain. Then vines and olives cover the terraces of limestone and earth. When the slope grows steeper, thick forests of oak and terebinth conceal the Master and his disciples.

He has spent the day in travel and in teaching, and this mountain climb at night adds a heavy weight to the weariness that demanded rest before the evening came. His hand has lifted the burden of infirmity from many shoulders, and sent the thrill of life into many a worn and wasted frame. But he himself is as much fatigued with the steep ascent as the impetuous Peter or the gentle John. They do not ask him whither he is going, or for what purpose he leads them away to the solitude of the mountain just as night is setting in, and they all need repose and protection in the homes which they have left behind. They have known him many times to spend the whole night in desert places, or upon lonely mountains in prayer, and they do not need to ask him for what purpose he leads them forth from the noisy crowd or the quiet homes of men at the evening hour. They go because he asks their company; and yet they think it strange that he must needs add this lonely watching in the chill air of night, to the weariness and exhaustion of the day. Peter thinks he is beside himself, and he would tell him so if he had not been so recently rebuked and silenced for obtruding advice upon his Master.

They reach the utmost height and look forth upon the world which they have left behind. It is a goodly sight to behold, and such an one as cannot be seen elsewhere in all the Holy

Land. Far away in the west, the waves of the Mediterranean glow, like molten gold, where the sun has sunk beneath the horizon. Northeast, Tiberias, the pearl of seas, lies deep-set among hills, with a changing border of golden tints and purple shadows; now calm, as if still sleeping beneath the spell of the mighty word that spoke peace to its stormy waves. Northward the snows of still loftier mountains look like altar-fires, burning unto the midst of heaven. Nearer, within the sweep of the eye, is the blessed Mount on which Jesus opened the ministry of reconciliation with beatitudes upon the poor, the meek and the merciful. Eastward, the highlands of Gilead and Bashan rise in broken ridges and rounded domes, like the waves of a stormy sea. Southward winds a silvery haze, marking the course where the swift Jordan rushes down its deep and rocky bed. Northwest, Carmel pushes out its bold headland into the sea, clothed with the excellency of the forest, and lifting itself up like an altar for the evening sacrifice, as in the day when the priests of Baal cried in vain to the god of fire to kindle his own offering, and the fire of the Lord fell at the word of Elijah.

The road where the prophet ran before the chariot of Ahab, in the face of a driving storm, up the vale of Esdraelon from Carmel to Jezreel; the wild hill-track, along which doomed and despairing Saul rode by night, from Endor, where he had been to seek forbidden knowledge, to Gilboa, where he went to fight and die; the harvest fields, where the only child of the Shunamite received a sun-stroke while watching the reapers; the stone houses of Shunem, where Elisha found the dead child in his own chamber and raised him to life; the hill-town of Nain, where Jesus stopped the funeral procession, and restored the dead son alive to his mother; despised Nazareth, where the Divine Life was hidden for thirty years, and Cana, imbosomed in orchards of pomegranates and reclined on the slope of a hill, where Jesus manifested forth his glory by the beginning of miracles; all are in sight. Plains of the greatest fertility, scenes of the deepest historic interest, mountains of the wildest and most desolate grandeur in all Palestine, may be seen from this one solitary height where Jesus goes apart with his three favored disciples, to spend the night in prayer.

But not to gaze on the landscape which one might travel half round the globe to see; not to rest after long and exhausting toil; not to escape impending danger, has Jesus sought this mountain solitude. He has no bed but the bare earth. The dew falls like rain at evening, and the morning wind will come from perpetual snows. To such a place the Man of sorrows goes to spend the whole night in prayer. And as his supplication continues hour after hour, with strong crying and many tears, the disciples grow weary with watching and they fall asleep. The midnight passes, and they sleep on, forgetful of their waking and agonizing Master.

He has told them of the great woe that will come upon him before another summer begins. They have only tried to divert his mind from such gloomy anticipations; and now, when he has taken them aside that they may watch with him while he prays for strength to meet the terrible conflict, they sleep as they slept again in Gethsemane, leaving him to bear his great agony alone. Their indifference must have been the more distressing to him for the reason that he was praying especially for such a manifestation of his glory before their eyes as would heal their unbelief, and help them to be reconciled to the humiliation and death which awaited him at Jerusalem.

And the mighty Mediator is not left to pray unheard. Suddenly, as if the golden gates of heaven had been thrown wide, and the splendor of the eternal throne had been poured upon the holy mount, the bending supplicant is clothed with a glory above the brightness of the sun. No longer prostrate in an agony of prayer, he seems to sit enthroned amid the radiance of light ineffable. His countenance wears the aspect of serene and godlike majesty, and his garments shine like the drifted snow beneath the noonday sun.

The sleeping disciples are wakened by the flood of glory covering the whole mount. Gazing with wonder and alarm upon the shining robes and the changed countenance of their Master, they see that he is not alone. The great lawgiver, who conversed with Jehovah amid the thunders and the darkness of Sinai, and the mighty prophet who was taken up in a chariot of fire, have come down from their heavenly rest to pay their homage to their King, and to talk with him of the appointed completion of his mission, while his disciples sleep. Somehow, strangely, they see at once that it is Moses and Elijah with whom he speaks. And these ancient worthies are fully aware of the awful tragedy to be accomplished at Jerusalem, the announcement of which from the lips of their Master had so greatly tasked their faith and afflicted their hearts.

The disciples are confused and bewildered by the sudden waking and by the awful vision. They know not what to say, and yet Peter, as usual, feels that he must speak. He repeats substantially, in a milder form, the suggestion for which he had already been severely rebuked by the meek and gentle Master. He proposes that Jesus shall remain at a safe distance from the dangers of Jerusalem and the death of the cross, and set up his throne, for the government of the world, upon that holy mount, and inaugurate his reign with the splendors with which they are surrounded.

And while he is yet speaking, the awful cloud of the Shechinah's glory that went before the tribes in the wilderness, overshadows them, and out of the cloud comes the divine voice which had spoken from the tabernacle of Moses and from the temple of Solomon. It sets at naught the weakness and vanity of all human counsel, and commands attention to the supreme source of wisdom and authority, saying, "This is my beloved Son. Hear him." And with that first and final lesson for the interpretation of all mysteries and the attainment of all faith, the vision passes. When the disciples, smitten to the ground by the terror of "the voice from the excellent glory," lift up their eyes again, they see no man but Jesus only.

The morning breaks upon the mountain with a brightness less than the vision of the night, and the returning day reveals a world of sin and suffering where Jesus and his disciples must resume the work of instruction and mercy. They have heard his divinity proclaimed by the voice from the unapproachable glory, and now they must follow him, in patience and faith, to the cross and the grave.

And for what purpose were the disciples called to witness and to record this extraordinary scene on the mount of the Transfiguration? Doubtless its full meaning must pass beyond our comprehension, as it did beyond theirs. Nevertheless it teaches some lessons which are as clear and important to us as they were to them.

It shows the suffering and glorified Redeemer to be the one object of supreme interest and attraction in the whole revelation of God to man. This meek and lowly Jesus, who, for two years and a half had been going to and fro a homeless wanderer through all Judæa, is disclosed on the holy mount as the son of the Highest, to whom the patriarchs and prophets of the olden time render homage, in whom the mighty spirits of the blessed world recognize their King. The great lawgiver of Israel, after fifteen hundred years of growing knowledge in the life of heaven, comes down from the mansions of paradise to acknowledge the divine Prophet and Deliverer, whose coming he had foretold so long ago. Moses himself is seen and heard reverently talking with Jesus of the great event of his crucifixion, in which the inhabitants of earth and heaven have the most profound and awful interest.

The greatest of all the prophets, whose presence was a terror to kings and whose prayers shut up heaven in the days of Israel's apostacy, comes back to acknowledge Jesus as a greater prophet than himself, and to speak of his appointed death in Jerusalem as the great expiation without which there could be no hope for a lost world. This august embassy from the world of spirits, representing all the providences and revelations in the past, and all the sublime intelligence of the redeemed in heaven, appears in glory on the holy mount, to testify, that in Christ, all promises of mercy to man are fulfilled, and that through his death only can there be redemption for the lost. The decease, which Christ was to accomplish at Jerusalem, was already known to the inhabitants of heaven. They speak of it as an event which must of necessity take place, and one which, in its consequences, would become the wonder of angels and the source of joy and praise to the universe.

That great event, so dark, so inexplicable, when foretold to the disciples, has now, for eighteen hundred years, become a matter of history, and it is the source of light, of joy and of blessing to millions to-day. The burden of sin, crushing the penitent and weary soul, falls at the foot of the cross. The afflicted and sorrowing are all comforted when they look to the cross. The darkness of the grave is scattered by the light which shines from the cross. We can glory and rejoice in every condition of life, we can triumph over death, just because the Son of God came down from heaven, took upon himself our infirmities, and voluntarily submitted to the sacrifice which his own disciples were most anxious to have him escape.

He has returned to his heavenly throne with the scars of his earthly conflict still upon him. While worshipped by adoring hosts, he still appears to them as one that has been slain. Our earthly worship will be most like that of heaven when most we exalt the sin-atoning Lamb. We shall be most sure of joining the society and the song of the blessed when most humbly and fully we trust in a crucified Saviour.

No one will understand the Gospel, who fails to see that the cross is the central source of hope, of life and of exaltation to man. No one will find peace in believing, so long as he is ashamed to bear the cross and follow Christ. No one will appreciate the blessing which the Gospel bestows, until he feels that he can richly and joyfully afford to sacrifice everything else only to win Christ and be found in him. Everything given for Christ enriches the giver, and everything suffered for him increases the final joy.

The transfiguration shows it to be our first and supreme duty to hear and obey Christ. The voice which gave this command on the holy mount, is the voice that Adam heard in Paradise. It speaks in the inspiration of the Psalms and the Prophets, and it declares our individual duty with the same authority by which the law was given to Moses, and judgments were inflicted by the word of Elijah. It directs every perplexed and doubting mind to Christ, saying evermore, "This is my beloved Son, hear him." It says to the guilty, the wretched and the hopeless, "Behold the Lamb of God that taketh away the sin of the world." It invites the weary and the heavy-laden to look to him for rest. It bids the thoughtless, the impenitent and the disobedient hear his words as he cries, "Except ye repent ye shall all likewise perish."

The voice of prophecy, the voice of the evangelists, the voice of the whole Bible, the voice of providence, the voice of conscience is ever directing to Christ and commanding all to hear and obey him. Christ himself, in his word, and life, and work, is the divine Wisdom which cries to men evermore for their instruction. He speaks alike to the mind that reasons, to the heart that feels and to the conscience which responds to the claims of obligation. He has a message of duty, of hope and of salvation for every soul. He has a right to command, and yet he condescends to entreat. He has the power to crush, and yet he waits to be gracious, he longs to forgive. He walked upon the waves; he hushed the storm; he healed the sick; he gave sight to the blind; he raised the dead; and all to show his power, his authority and his willingness to save the soul.

He still confers the gifts of health and instruction, and Sabbaths, and sanctuaries, and countless providential blessings, that he may make us willing to hear his voice when he speaks of things of infinite and everlasting interest to us all. He would kindle the feeblest love into deathless flame; he would inspire the faintest heart with immortal hope. He would make the least and poorest kings unto God. He alone can answer the one question of greatest moment to every human being in the world, "What must I do to be saved?"

Jesus himself, the greatest of teachers, the regenerator of the human mind, the Saviour of the human soul, speaks in the language of common life. He communicates the lessons of heavenly wisdom in such terms as appeal to the experience and necessities of all. He adapts his instruction to all times and places, to all classes and conditions of men. The humble synagogue without a seat, the fishing boat rocking on the wave, the sand of the seashore, the greensward of the mountain-side, the solitude of the desert, the highway thronged with travelers, the princely mansion crowded with guests, the private house where the homeless wanderer rests for the night, the streets and public squares of the city, the sacred courts of the temple with men coming and going all the while, are his places of preaching and the pulpit from which he proclaims truths to shake the world.

He speaks always upon the greatest themes that can ever engage the mind of man, and yet he presents them in such a form as to instruct the loftiest intellect and interest the feeblest understanding. An honest desire to know the way of life is the best qualification to learn of him who spake as never man spake. Become as a little child, conscious of weakness and willing to be instructed, and you will easily learn from the divine Teacher a higher wisdom than was ever taught in the most renowned schools of human philosophy. Receive the word of Christ as a personal message to your own heart; appropriate to yourself the merits of his death as fully as if you were the only sinner in the world for whom he died, and you will easily learn how to be saved.

It is the first duty and the highest honor of the preacher to stand and point the way to Jesus, and say, "Behold the Lamb of God, who taketh away the sin of the world." Everything in his manner and thought and speech and life, should be a living interpretation of the voice from the excellent glory, "This is my beloved Son, hear ye him." The highest recommendation of the gospel from human lips, is that which most clearly presents Christ lifted up on the cross as the supreme object of attraction and desire, drawing all men unto himself. It is in hearing Christ that we display the highest wisdom; it is in following Christ that we choose the noblest part; it is in obeying Christ that we secure our eternal salvation.

The transfiguration shows how intimate the relation which exists between this every day life of ours and the spiritual world. Jesus and his three disciples had talked and traveled and wearied themselves on the day preceding the ascent of the holy mount, just as we work and weary ourselves in our daily occupations. The mountain which they climbed at evening, was high and steep and cold, shadowed by clouds, bathed in sun-light, swept by storms, shrouded in darkness, just like the mountains which we have seen, just like the hills which we have climbed. When the night came on, the landscape of vineyards and fields and villages beneath them faded into darkness; the solemn stars looked down from the silent sky, and the earth and rocks beneath them were wet with dews, just as the night now comes in desert places.

And yet it was to them, on that lonely height, living, breathing men like ourselves, that there appeared from the spiritual world other men who had lived a thousand years before. These men, Moses and Elijah, appeared so truly the same that they were centuries before, that the disciples knew them simply from having read their history. They did not seem to have come from afar. The glory that burst forth from the person of Jesus appeared only to have shown the disciples a presence that was with them unseen before: The veil was lifted from their eyes and they saw with what companionship they were surrounded, and in the midst of what unseen and glorious presences they were walking wherever they went in the company of Jesus. And so the peculiar manner in which Jesus is said by the evangelists to have shown himself to his disciples after his resurrection, implies that he was already with them and it was only necessary for their eyes to be opened to behold him in the midst of their company.

To all who believe in Jesus now, there are times when it seems as if the spiritual world were all around them, and they can almost feel the touch of unseen hands, extended to lead them on in safety, when perils and difficulties beset the way. Sometimes they feel themselves to be covered by the overshadowing of angels' wings, and ministered unto by the presence and sympathies of unseen comforters. The chamber of death, where the disciple of Jesus dies, sometimes seems to shine with an unearthly light, to catch the sound of heavenly harmonies, to be kept, through the long hours of weariness and pain, by unseen watchers.

There may be something of fancy in all this. But it is nevertheless good for us to believe, that the realities of the unseen world are very near, and that the departed disciples of Jesus are in active sympathy with those, whose season of trial and of temptation is not yet closed. In every sacrifice we make for Jesus, in every burden we bear for him, it is good for us to feel that we are serving a King, whose face our beloved and blessed dead are permitted to behold, and with whom they speak in reverent and holy communion, as Moses and Elijah talked with him on the mount of the Transfiguration. And so may we cultivate in our hearts a purer and a more constant longing, ourselves also to appear with him in glory on the holy mount of Paradise.

The Transfiguration teaches us that the loftiest visions of faith and joy, are given to fit us for the struggles and temptations of our daily life. From the mount of the excellent glory, from the midst of the opened heavens, and the companionship of the blessed, Jesus went down to a world of tears and sufferings, to renew his struggle with the unbelief and perversity of men, to take up again the burden of their guilt and sorrow, and bear it to the cross and the grave.

These two utmost extremes of glory and of grief, the heavenly transfiguration and the earthly toil and sorrow, are combined in one representation by Raphael, in his last and greatest work,—many would say the greatest painting of all masters and of all times,—on which the world has gazed with wonder and admiration for three hundred years. Christ himself is seen on the mount, radiant with light, reposing in serene and gentle majesty upon the viewless air, as he once walked upon the wave. There has been but one human hand, that could represent to the eye, such benignity and grace, such effulgence of glory as shine in that wondrous countenance. Moses and Elijah are rapt in ecstacies of love and adoration, as they gaze upon the living and embodied radiance of love divine. Beneath, the three disciples, shielding their eyes with their hands from the blinding splendor poured from the person of their Master, have fallen upon the ground, unable to look on his face, and yet less able to cease from gazing.

At the foot of the mount is seen the lunatic child, with distorted and deathlike countenance, gnashing his teeth and convulsed with agony; the father imploring help from the disciples, the mother seconding the appeal, with the pangs of a broken heart in every look, the scribes cavilling, the physicians closing the books which they have consulted in vain for a cure, and the disciples themselves perplexed and in despair.

And all this unbelief and helplessness, this suffering and sorrow among men, at the very foot of the mountain, on which the Son of God is revealed in glory, to take on himself the burdens and iniquities of a lost world. The great master of pictorial representation, violates some of the minor rules of his art, for the sake of securing a higher moral effect. He presents the divine glory of the Redeemer and the guilt and misery of man, in one view, that the silent lesson of the twofold scene, may encourage all the wretched and sinful to look up for help, and that it may teach all who share in the vision of faith and joy, to come down from the lofty heights of devotion and communion with Christ, to instruct the ignorant, to help the needy and to save the lost.

It is good, at times, to put the wickedness and the misery of the world, at the farthest possible remove from our thoughts, and give ourselves wholly, to the peace and blessedness, with which the presence of Christ fills the believing heart. It is good to retire from the busy scenes of life, and gaze with wonder and adoration, upon the glory of Christ, and feast the soul with the raptures of assured faith and perfect love.

But the "vision of the King," and the foretaste of heaven will not come at our bidding. It is in the common walks of duty, that we are most sure of meeting Jesus in the way. The lowliest home may receive angel guests, and the most weary pilgrim may drink of the fountain of life. There are toils and conflicts and self-denials for us all to meet. There must needs be tears and sorrows for many sins:

struggles and watchings for the mastery of depraved desires and dispositions, offerings and consecrations, submissions and sacrifices that seem like taking the life blood from the heart. There must be persevering effort to do good, and patient waiting for success, and earnest supplication for others, that will not give them up to be lost.

And when by such steps we have climbed the holy mount of faith, and seen the face of Jesus in his glory, we must go again into all the haunts and homes of men to testify of the vision, that others may be drawn to see its light and share its joy. The purest and loftiest devotion, is that which breathes forth in the most earnest desire and effort to bring all souls to Jesus, and to secure the salvation of all through him. The glory of the Transfiguration is a passing gleam of heaven's light, cast upon the pathways of earth, to draw our hearts to that land, where there is no night, and to that home where there are no tears.

JERICHO.

As he went out of Jericho with his disciples and a great number of people, blind Bartimæus, the son of Timæus, sat by the highway-side begging. And when he heard that it was Jesus of Nazareth, he began to cry out, and say, Jesus, thou son of David, have mercy on me.—MARK x. 46, 47.

VI.
JERICHO.

ANCIENT CASTLE NEAR JERICHO.

AT Jericho, outside of the city gate, on the road leading to Jerusalem, and consequently most thronged with travelers, sits the blind Bartimæus, begging. The poorest of the many poor who cry for bread in all the cities and highways of Judea, he has blindness added to poverty, that his cup of misery may run over. To him the whole of life is one long deep night, to which there is no return of morn, no visitation from the glory and the gladness of God's blessed light. There is no flower in all the fields which opens on him with its eye of beauty; he sees no smile of pity or of recognition in the "human face divine." The heavens above him are one thick cloud, through which no star shines; the earth, spread out for other eyes to behold, with all its gladdening hills, and grassy plains, and laughing streams, to him is nothing but solid and substantial darkness.

Placed in the midst of a landscape as various and enchanting as any on which the sun shines in all its course, he lives in the midst of a darkness which shuts him in as with an impenetrable wall on every side. Whether morning comes on golden wings from the gorgeous East, or the sun flames from his mid-day throne, or evening brings forth its troop of stars upon the plains of heaven, it is all night to him. His darkened eye-balls roll in vain to find the lost day. His imprisoned soul yearns in vain to find some way out of the thick gloom and the shadow of death with which he is surrounded.

It has not always been so with him; for he could once see. And the remembrance of the beauty and the glory with which God covers the hills of Judea in the blossoming spring and the ripening summer, and which he could once behold, deepens, by contrast, the darkness with which he is surrounded. And, what adds greatly to his misery, he has been taught by the doctrines and traditions of his countrymen, that blindness has been inflicted upon him in distinction from the rest of men, as an especial judgment for his sins. He must believe that the great Father of light, whose smile fills the universe with beauty and with blessing, only frowns on him with the thick clouds of his anger. The ignorant peasant and the learned priest alike tell him that it is for his sins that he has been left to grope his way to the grave, which cannot be darker than the sightless sepulchre in which his soul is already buried.

And there he sits in such a case, feeling his way by the wall, as he comes every morning, depending on others to tell him when it is night, uncertain whether his wretched condition, and his supplicating cry, will stir enough of pity in the passing traveler, to secure him the means of prolonging his miserable life. Many pass without bestowing on him the pitiful boon of a morsel of food or a word of kindness. Many times the only alleviation which he obtains from the proud priest and the prouder Pharisee, is the severe and self-righteous assertion, that it becomes not man to bless with charity one whom God has cursed for his sins. Many times the idle vagabond, as wretched as himself, in everything but blindness, pauses a moment in passing to make mirth of his misery.

And so he must be looked upon by others, and he must look upon himself, while life lasts, as a living monument of heaven's vengeance on all transgressors of its sacred laws; himself a more pitiable and afflicting desolation than the blasted plain of Sodom, towards which the swift Jordan flows within sight of his native city. There is no power in the touch or the skill of the physician, to restore to his darkened eye-balls their lost sensibility to heaven's light. No human hand can draw back the thick veil with which blindness has covered the universe to him as with the pall of death.

And yet within the last two years, from time to time, a most strange and exciting report has come to his ears. Occasionally some one passer-by, more kindly and commiserating than the rest, has paused by his side, and in addition to his trifling gift, has delayed to tell him of One possessing the power to open the eyes of the blind with a single word. He hears that that wonderful personage is ever going from city to city, in other portions of Judea, performing such miraculous cures for the afflicted, and even raising the dead to life. Of late the fame of his mighty works has come nearer, and has been accredited by more numerous witnesses. And blind Bartimæus, ever sitting by the way-side, begging, has even begun to hope that the Friend of the friendless might some day pass in or out at the gate of Jericho, and in passing, graciously pour the light of day again on him.

Often has he thought that he would gladly

travel to the utmost boundary of Palestine, if he could thus secure the opportunity, for one moment, to lift up his supplicating cry for help within the hearing of the divine Deliverer. All the riches in the world would be as nothing to him in comparison with one word of healing power from that mighty and merciful friend of the needy. He begins to suspect that this extraordinary person may be the promised Son of David, the Deliverer of Israel, of whom the Prophet spoke; and what interests him still more, he is said to be the Friend of sinners; he seeks the guilty and the outcast; he speaks to them with words of kindness and encouragement, and freely displays his miraculous power in their behalf.

Be it so, then, as he has been often told, that his blindness is the curse of God on him for his sins; still, in the Friend of sinners he might venture to hope. He would not be spurned by one who cleansed the loathsome leper of an uncleanness which corrupted the body, because it had first polluted the soul. He would not be scorned by one who cast out the foul spirit from those who had been possessed by the demons of darkness for their wickedness. He who never shrunk from contact with the vilest, if by approaching them he could do them good—surely he would not say of blind Bartimæus, "Behold one cursed of God for his sins," and shaking his garments, pass on his way more rapidly to avoid the sight and the touch of such pollution.

And yet, often as he has listened with eager attention to the tales told him, by delaying travelers, of the mighty works done by Jesus of Nazareth, he has only thus learned the more bitterly and hopelessly to deplore his still continued blindness. He has long listened in vain for any announcement from the passing multitude that Jesus is among them. He has no kind friend to take him by the hand, and lead him away to those favored portions of Judea, where the Friend of sinners may be found ready to heal the humblest applicant for his aid. He can do naught but sit here by the gate of Jericho with the feeble and uncertain hope that perchance the Prophet of Nazareth may pass that way and have compassion on him.

And so it comes to pass at last that on a certain day, blind Bartimæus hears the sound of an unusual multitude and the murmur of many voices pressing along the public way, and coming near the gate of the city where he sits. And when he inquires the meaning of the strange sound, he is told that "Jesus of Nazareth passeth by." Now, then, at last has come his first, it may be his last opportunity to recover his lost sight. Now, if ever, must the pall of darkness be lifted from him, and he shall behold again the magnificence of the blue heavens, and the beauty of the green earth, and he shall read again in the silent looks of the human face the unutterable things of the soul.

How priceless the value of the single opportunity presented to blind Bartimæus by the passing of Jesus of Nazareth this one day. The mighty Helper of the needy is within hearing but a few moments, and when gone may never return again. How much deeper will be the darkness of future years to the blind, if he shall have it to remember that once his eyes might have been opened, but he failed to ask.

And yet it may cost something to gain a gift which may be had for asking. This man has been named and pointed at with horror by the most religious of his countrymen as accursed of God. And shall he presume that the holy prophet of Nazareth will be more indulgent towards his sins than his friends and neighbors? May it not be that the reports which have come to his ears, concerning the healing power of Jesus, are all exaggerations? If he asks so strange a thing as that his eyes may be opened, will it not expose him to the mockery of the multitude, and so deprive him of the meagre support which comes from their pity and charity? Were it not wiser to improve this opportunity, only to make more careful inquiry concerning Jesus, and if satisfactory evidence of his divine power and benignity should be secured, be prepared at another time to seek his aid? The most learned and religious of his countrymen have said that this Jesus is a deceiver and a fanatic. If he should ask the performance of a miraculous work from such an one, would he not renounce faith in God, and bring on himself a worse evil than blindness?

Thus, a cautious and distrustful man might easily have spent, in hesitancy or consideration, the few moments while Jesus was passing, and so lost forever an opportunity, which, when gone, he would give everything in the world to gain once more. There is no madness like that which pauses to reason, when the destiny of the soul depends upon immediate and decisive action.

But blind Bartimæus, at the gate of Jericho, is guilty of no such considerate folly as this. He wastes no time in studying proprieties of speech or attitudes of supplication. It is enough for him to know that Jesus of Nazareth passeth by. He asks only for such help as can be given to the guilty, for he asks for mercy. He assumes, safely and unhesitatingly, that the mercy of Jesus will be enough for him. And he lifts up his cry with a determination that will not be put to silence by the rebukes of the multitude, or the apparent inattention of Jesus himself.

When told, at last, that Jesus stops in the way and calls him, he rises, casts aside his garment, that he may be the freer to run, rushes in his blindness without waiting to be led in the direction of the divine Helper whom he cannot see. He is ready to risk everything, only to hear one word of hope from that voice which can speak the dead to life. And when told to name the act of mercy which he would have done for him, he shows the strength of his faith by asking that which divine power alone can do.

And, as of old, there was needed only one omnific word, and light sprang into being; so Jesus speaks the word "SEE," and blind Bartimæus receives his sight, and follows him in the way, praising and rejoicing. That one word of Jesus rolls back the darkness with which the universe had been covered to the blind, and creates for him a new world of light and life, and surpassing glory. The long night of years is past, and the resplendent noon of recovered sight has flashed upon him, without waiting for the slow approaches of the breaking day.

And now he sees, not simply with the restored sensibility of the bodily eye, but with "the vision and faculty divine" of faith in the

Son of God. The restored world on which he now looks with unutterable joy, is to him not simply the one which he lost with the loss of sight. In the ecstacy of his new joy it seems to him as if it were Paradise restored. The sunlight rests upon it with a glorious and loving beauty, as if it were the smile of God on pronouncing his new creation very good, and its many voices sound, to the recovered blind man, like the echo of that one word of Jesus by which his eyes were opened. The power of that mighty word has poured light upon the soul as well as upon the eye; the infinite love which gave it utterance has set up its throne in his heart, and made him a new creature in the image of God.

He can now find nothing but mercy in the awful affliction which he had been taught to regard only as a curse. For it has been by the blindness of the eye that spiritual light has found entrance to the darker chambers of the soul. Were he now to lose again, beyond recovery, the sight of the bodily eye, still so much the more would the celestial light of the divine love shine inward upon the soul, and he would still continue to live in a new spiritual creation, illumined all over with heaven's holy light. And all this blessed experience of unutterable joy, this deliverance from a universe of darkness and a destiny of despair, bestowed upon one poor benighted and most afflicted soul, in answer to his first believing prayer unto Him who is the light of the world.

We see no more the face of the Son of Man. No tidings come to tell us of his mighty works in any land. No curious multitude gather to hear him in desert places, or in the busy streets. No voices are heard by the way-side or at city gates, saying, "Jesus of Nazareth passeth by." And yet, for all the practical purposes of his redeeming work, Christ is still in the world. He still walks unseen through all our streets; he comes on the message of mercy to all our homes; he stands ready to breathe his loving Spirit into every heart. He is ever passing by in the ministrations of his grace, with the power to deliver all souls from the darkness of unbelief, and from the destiny of despair. The deep sense of need which no riches of the earth can relieve; the sigh of penitence which never finds utterance on the lip; the longing for peace which the world can never satisfy, are all known to him. By such experiences, he puts to every soul the question which he put to the blind at the gate of Jericho, "What wilt thou that I should do unto thee?"

The gospel of Jesus, from beginning to end, is pervaded with the one distinctive and controlling idea,—help for the needy, light for the blind, redemption for the lost. And Jesus himself comes, in all the ministrations of his Spirit and his word, to bring this freely offered grace, this full and everlasting salvation, within reach of every soul. No human tongue can describe, no finite mind can conceive the value of one opportunity to sit where Jesus of Nazareth passeth by. How great then the privilege of those to whom that mighty Helper comes, morning, evening, and at noon of day, saying, "What wilt thou that I should do unto thee?"

Along all the highways of life, there are many blind, groping for the lost day, and finding it not. Blind to their own interest, they gather dust with their busy hands, and think themselves rich. Blind to their own danger, they walk upon the brink of perdition, and think it safe. Blind to their own happiness, they lay up for themselves regret and sorrow, and call it pleasure. Blind to their own conduct, they disown and dishonor the greatest Friend they have in the universe, and say—we mean no harm, we have done no wrong. Blind to their own destiny, they live for earth and time alone, and leave the endless future to take care of itself. To all the higher interests of the soul, to all the blessed and glorious prospects of life beyond the grave, the anxious, burdened, gain-seeking children of this world, are utterly blind. They labor for that which satisfieth not; they spend their money for that which is not bread; they strive in vain to content themselves with pleasures and possessions which must perish when their real existence has only just begun.

To them in such a condition, Jesus comes. He offers to do for them that which they need most to have done; to bestow on them a blessing which all the treasures of the earth would not be rich enough to buy: to give them a peace and a hope which would be infinite gain if it cost them the toils and the sufferings of a whole life. In their dark and unsatisfactory condition, having no hope and without God in the world, they seldom think how often Jesus of Nazareth passeth by; how often he stands before them in the ways, ready to pour the light of heaven's peace and joy and rest into their weary souls. Not only is the offer of his grace constant and free; it is often pressed upon reason with arguments of mighty power; it is often urged home upon conscience with the solemnity of eternal judgment to confirm the appeal, insomuch that one must be utterly hardened in his worldliness and unbelief not to cry out with a bursting heart, "Jesus, Lord, have mercy on me."

Sometimes he touches the heart with a new tenderness to the appeals of his own word; sometimes he quickens the feeling of obligation into new life; sometimes he burdens the soul with the utter wretchedness of living and dying without a Saviour; and in all such experiences, he comes especially nigh. Whoever

Site of Jericho, with the only remaining Stone Building on the right.

permits such a tenderness of heart to the power of truth to subside into coldness and indifference, commits a greater wrong against himself than he would if he should decline the offer of the highest crown on earth.

When God's afflicting providence darkens the household with the shadow of death, and the grave takes to its cold bosom one that was bound to the living with the strongest bonds of love, then the suffering Saviour comes with the offer of his own divine sympathy to heal the deepest sorrow, and to make the sorest bereavement the greatest blessing. Whoever, in such bereavement, looks only to man for consolation, or plunges into the vortex of business or pleasure to dissipate his grief, turns away from the only Friend who can give peace to the soul.

When disappointment reveals the vanity of all earthly things; when the fear of death passes like a shadow over the spirit; when preparation for eternity seems for the moment the first and the only true work of life, then is Jesus of Nazareth passing by; then is the door of the kingdom of heaven thrown open for the weary to enter and find rest. Nobody can tell how common or trifling a circumstance the Divine Spirit may employ to show men their need of redemption, and the nearness of him who alone can save.

It may be a solitary thought that takes possession of the mind in a wakeful hour at midnight; it may be a tone, a look, a word suddenly armed with a mysterious and irresistible power to sway the heart and to control every feeling; it may be the repetition of an argument, a warning, a cry of alarm which has been heard a hundred times before without effect; it may be the remembrance of slighted counsel faithfully given in other years, or the vivid anticipation of an hour when counsel can no longer be of any avail; any, or all such circumstances, and a thousand others, may be the voice which says, "Jesus of Nazareth passeth by." To have been drawn to Christ by one such influence; to have had one clear, strong impression of his nearness and willingness to save, is a blessing of more value than all the riches and pleasures and glories of earth and time

And shall any one suffer such blessed influences to come and go as if they were trifles light as air? Nay, rather let all to whom the message of life comes, tenderly cherish every impression from any source which deepens the sense of need, and at the same time awakens the conviction that Christ is near to save.

The slightest inclination to heed the high claims of religion, to lay hold on the offered inheritance of eternal life, is too sacred and precious a thing to be trifled with for a moment. No question better deserves the attention of an earnest man than this one, "What shall I do to be saved?" They are only voices of temptation and falsehood which would hush that inquiry by saying, "Why so much alarmed? what need of fear when there is no sign of danger? Life is long, the pleasures and cares of the present are enough, without burdening the heart with anxiety for the future. And, besides, the Saviour is always near, and peace with God can better be made in the dying hour."

Many such voices will come to bid the anxious inquirer "hold his peace." But they are false. They never satisfy. They can never save. They can be listened to only at the peril of the soul. They can be obeyed only at the hazard of eternal life. If it were the last counsel given to a troubled, sin-burdened soul, upon the very borders of the eternal world, in full view of the account which the living and the dying must give to God, nothing less than this could be said, "Go to Jesus, and without delay. Whoever bids you hold your peace, whatever hindrances keep you back, go to Jesus, and without delay."

BETHANY.

Bethany was nigh unto Jerusalem, about fifteen furlongs off. And he went out of the city into Bethany and lodged there. Now a certain man was sick, named Lazarus, of Bethany, the town of Mary and her sister Martha.—JOHN xi. 1-18: MATT. xxi. 17.

VII.
BETHANY.

 HALF hour's walk eastward from the wall of Jerusalem, across the Kidron valley, past Gethsemane and over the ridge of Olivet, brings one to Bethany. All the way the eye rests upon scenes which Jesus saw; the foot treads upon ground once hallowed

by the blessed feet of the Son of God. In all his visits to Jerusalem, he entered the city in the morning, spent the day in works of instruction and mercy, and then at evening, went out to find a congenial home for the night, on the mount of Olives. Sometimes he rested at the house of a friend, among the orchards and gardens on the western slope facing the city. And then he would often spend the late hours of the night in the open air, alone, or in tender communion with his favorite disciples. Sometimes he would pass over the ridge to the eastern descent, to find a ready welcome at one favored house, in this lonely mountain village of Bethany.

Here he was more completely shut out from all the world. The steep wall of the mountain rose up between him and the city. The wild and desolate hamlet itself stood upon a rugged platform of rock. The slopes around were faced with broad ledges of naked limestone, and scattered fragments of gray rock, interspersed here and there with silvery olive and dark green fig-trees. The outlook eastward was through a narrow glen, down the dreary and dangerous road to Jericho, and over the desolate wilderness of Judea, and across the wild gorge of the Jordan, with the rocky wall of the mountains of Moab beyond. The little village was crowded close upon the side of a narrow glen; an intervening ridge cut off the view of the top of Olivet from behind, and beyond there was not a sign of a human dwelling in sight in any direction.

This secluded and solitary town was not known to history, till it became the nightly resting-place of our Lord; but it was so intimately connected with the closing scenes of his earthly life, that Bethany shall be a name of peace and of blessing, long as the Gospel lives in the world. Taking the inspired record for our guide, let us retire to this lonely mountain village, and revive the sacred memories which gather around the home where Jesus came as a welcome guest.

1. THE NAME.

The first that we know of the town, it is mentioned as the home of the family that Jesus loved; and to this day, it bears the name of one whom Jesus raised from the dead. Even in his time, the sacred historian gave the village its most lasting and honorable distinction, by naming it from the single house where Jesus lodged at night. That lonely rock-built hamlet, walled in by the mountain, and looking forever upon the desert, shall have a blessed memorial through all coming ages, because one of its humble homes afforded shelter and hospitality to him who had not where to lay his head.

We make pilgrimages to the birth-place of heroes. We count it a privilege to visit the walks and groves once frequented by the sages and masters in the world's philosophy. We look with awe upon the sculptured tomb where the dust of kings and conquerors is kept with religious veneration. We walk in silence and deep thought over the field where embattled nations met in the shock of arms, and the earthly destiny of millions was determined in a day. But neither sage, nor hero, nor king, nor battle could confer upon any place such sacred and lasting distinction as Bethany received from the house where Jesus went to rest at night.

The great events of time are objects of interest to the heavenly host. They know, better than we do, the scenes of earth around which cluster the most sacred and awful associations. As they pass from land to land and from nation to nation, with the swiftness of light, upon errands of judgment and of mercy, they learn a truer geography of great events than is ever taught in earthly schools. But we can hardly think of them as saying to each other, "In such a town was born the conqueror of nations, whose phalanx swept the armies of the East as withered leaves are swept before the storm; on this ruin-covered hill the Cæsars kept their imperial state; beneath yonder dome rest the ashes of one, the thunder of whose cannon echoed from the Nile to the Niemen, to the march of whose legions all Europe trembled for twenty years."

It is a matter of far deeper interest to them, to trace the earthly steps of that mighty King who veiled the glory of heaven beneath the garb of a peasant and who asked entertainment for a night from creatures whom his own power had made. In their better judgment of the historic past, and the endless future in man's destiny, it is a fact of more fearful meaning, that a certain house in a lonely mountain village received the Son of God as a familiar and welcome guest.

Christ himself has gone back to his heavenly throne. But his spirit, enshrined and incarnate in his disciples, walks abroad through all the earth, and hallows for them the lowliest habitations. He shares the cave, the hovel, the dungeon, with those who suffer for his sake, and their places of abode, though unwritten in the world's geography, are inscribed in letters of light upon the enduring records of heaven. The inhabitants of other worlds shall visit the homes where the disciples of Jesus lived and suffered and died on this earth, when the palaces of kings and the monuments of heroes are forgotten.

There is many a miserable garret, many a damp cellar in the great city, many a lonely cabin in the open country, where God's mighty angels are daily visitants, because the Son of

God has been there before them to bless some poor, suffering disciple, and his presence has made the humble abode more glorious in their estimate, than all the splendors of earthly state.

Sometimes the princely mansion entertains the divine Guest in its meanest apartment, simply because some poor, tired servant, late at night, climbs up the many-storied stairs, and before lying down to rest consecrates that narrow chamber with fervent and grateful prayer. That great house is visited by messengers from heaven, just because its humblest inmate is an heir of salvation. The honored name which it bears, the splendors of art with which it is adorned, the courtly company with which it is thronged would have no attraction for them, if they did not find there one whom Jesus loves. To them paintings and sculpture and gorgeous robes and flashing gems are but dust and ashes; but in the faithful life of the lowliest and most despised servant of Christ, they see the dawn of endless glory and immortality. And the name of this lonely mountain village of Bethany shall be kept in everlasting and grateful remembrance, because it was the home of the family that Jesus loved.

2. THE GOOD PART.

The first visit of our Lord to the friendly house in Bethany, brings out the characters of the two sisters, Martha and Mary, in striking contrast with each other. He had come in from a weary walk of eight hours, up the steep, rugged and robber-haunted-road from Jericho, It was the time for the great multitude of pilgrims from Galilee to pass through the village on their way to Jerusalem to attend the feast of the Tabernacles. The house was thronged with guests coming and going early and late. When Jesus and his disciples appeared weary and exhausted with climbing up the long, steep ascent of the mountain path from the plain of the Jordan, the little family must have been thrown into some degree of excitement and anxiety in answering the unusual demands upon their hospitality.

Martha assumes the leading part, takes the place of mistress of the house, and is quite

beside herself with hurry and solicitude to provide for her guests. She thinks it the first duty to answer the physical wants of her divine Visitor, and then she may rest and delight herself with listening to his words. She is utterly surprised and indignant that any one of her family should expect the blessed Teacher to talk, hungry, weary and exhausted as he was, with eight hours of hard climbing up the steep and stony path from Jericho.

On the other hand, Mary, perhaps not more sincerely devoted to Jesus, but more quiet and contemplative in her disposition, forgets everything else in her desire to hear all that he would say. Leaving the domestic preparations to the care of her sister, she steals quietly into the apartment where the guests were gathered, seats herself at the feet of Jesus and listens with silent rapture to his gracious words. While there, she is missed by those of the family who are hurrying to prepare the needed entertainment for the hungry guests. The anxious and excited Martha suddenly bursts into the room and expresses, before all the company, her surprise and displeasure that Jesus himself should permit or approve such desertion of domestic duties. This impulsive and unseemly interruption drew from the lips of Jesus the memorable words, "Martha, Martha, thou art careful and troubled about many things; but one thing is needful and Mary hath chosen that good part, which shall not be taken away from her."

Now it is distinctly said in the sacred narrative, that Jesus loved each member of this family. The gentle and loving John, who was present on this occasion, gives no hint that Martha was less esteemed than Mary. Jesus did not reprove this excellent housekeeper and hospitable woman for the part of work and entertainment which she had generously chosen, but for her busy, bustling and talkative anxiety about many things which were only made worse by anxiety. He would not have her distract herself and family to hurry the preparations, or to load the table with ambitious abundance. He considered the unusual demands that were made upon her hospitality, by the arrival of so many weary and hungry guests, and he would have her take time to meet the demand with a quiet and cheerful mind.

The good part which Mary had chosen, was not simply the act of sitting at his feet and hearing his words, but the longing desire to receive what Christ alone could give, the words of eternal life. Martha is restless and troubled with her endeavors to make the entertainment worthy of the house and of the Guest; and she is displeased that her sister can pause in the midst of such hurry and excitement, and sit down quietly to hear the words of Jesus.

These two sisters of Bethany represent two phases of Christian character, everywhere springing from a like diversity in constitutional temperament. Both have their excellences within certain limits, and both exhibit defects when their ruling disposition is pressed to undue extremes. It should be our constant study to combine the calm and contemplative devotion of the one, with the energy and activity of the other. Great energy in action must needs be accompanied with great quietness of spirit, or it will soon exhaust itself in ineffectual struggles, and leave its work half done. If we would grow in wisdom and in usefulness, we must cultivate the capacity to listen and to learn, as well as to talk and to teach. There are times when speech and action are the first duty; and there are times when silence and contemplation are the most excellent virtues. The tendency of the present day is to give too much of a bustling and business aspect to our religion, and to neglect that inner spiritual cultivation, without which all outward show of zeal and activity rests upon an uncertain foundation.

The demand of the age is for men of action. And while there is much reason in that, it would be better if there were a greater demand for men of thought and devotion, men of conscience and faith. The two qualities should go together. The dark problems of the age will not be solved without much hard thinking and profound meditation. The most urgent work of the age will not be done without great physical endurance and unconquerable energy in action. The world needs quiet and contemplative Christians like gentle Melancthon and heavenly-minded Leighton and mystic Fenelon to teach the lesson of repose to weary hearts, and to lend the charm of quiet and thoughtful kindness to all the relations of private life. The world needs Christians of intense and impassioned natures like Augustine and Edwards and Brainerd to fathom the depths of their own spiritual necessities and to tell the terrible secrets of the soul in words of fire. And the world needs sons of thunder, Christians with nerves of iron and faces of adamant, like Luther and Knox and Cromwell, to shake the nations with their stormy vehemence, and to beat down the strongholds of iniquity with words that strike like battleaxes.

If these several characters cannot be combined in one person, it is better that they shall exist separately and in excess, than that the world shall lose the services of either. The quiet and passive virtues are beautiful and lovely at home, but they lack energy and daring for the conquest of the world. The restless activity and courage which overturns thrones and assaults iniquity in the strongholds of its power, and thunders round the earth with its great heroisms and victories, lacks the quietude and thoughtfulness requisite to the highest spiritual cultivation.

And we must not bring on ourselves the rebuke of the Master by blaming others, whose line of duty and of developement is different from our own. The world is large enough for us all to live in, and it has work enough for us all to do, and tasks suited to the tastes and capacities of each individual without giving any one occasion to say, either that he can do nothing or that his is the only way of doing anything. All diversities of the one human lot, all endowments of the one human mind, all denominations of the one Christian church, have suitable and honorable work to do, and it should be the ambition of all, in their appropriate sphere, to do the most and the best. Wherever we may see others led by sincere love to the Master, though it may be a different path from our own, let us not blame what he is sure to bless. Whether they engage in great public enterprises or sit in contemplation at his feet, whether they keep themselves much before the world or court retirement and repose, so long as each improves his own proper gift, let us concede the liberty of judgment to all, let us give offence to the conscience of none.

3. THE MEMORIAL.

On another occasion, our Lord received a special entertainment at Bethany, provided by the same friends and probably in the same house, in grateful commemoration of his great miracle in raising Lazarus from the dead. It was only six days before his crucifixion and he was on his way to Jerusalem, to meet the great sacrifice which awaited him there. At this time also the house was filled with guests, and there was great curiosity to see the man who had been waked to life, after having slept the sleep of death four days. While they were reclined at table, Mary took a pound of very precious ointment, and anointed the feet of Jesus and wiped his feet with the hair of her head. And when some exclaimed with indignation against such a costly expression of devotion, Jesus rebuked their complaints with these memorable words, "Verily, I say unto you, wherever this gospel shall be preached in the whole world, there shall also this, that this woman hath done, be told for a memorial of her."

This is the only promise of the kind that Jesus ever made, and this Mary is the only woman in all the past, with respect to whom we have a divine assurance that her fame and the influence of her life shall fill the world, and endure through all time. When Cleopatra of Egypt, and Zenobia of Palmyra, and Catharine of Russia are forgotten, or are remembered only to be pitied and despised, Mary of Bethany shall be honored with loving and grateful devotion.

Eighteen hundred years have passed since this promise was given, and already the name and humble service of this retiring woman have become known to a greater number of persons than any woman's name to be found in all profane history. The brief story of her life has been read and heard with profound interest by countless millions. Her affecting testimonial of love to Jesus has touched the fountain of tears, and brought millions of offerings to the poor for whom the wasteful parsimony of the disciples would have kept her gift. The one act of consecrating and sacramental devotion, into which she poured her whole weeping and passionate soul of love, has done more to make the human heart a sanctuary for the indwelling of holy love, than all ever done by the proud daughters of princes, or the worshipped stars of beauty in imperial courts.

And this woman of Bethany was not in the least indebted to riches, or rank, or personal accomplishments for the blessed memory that crowns and beautifies her name in all Christian annals. She was not a king's daughter. She had not learned the accomplishments of refined and cultivated society. She could not boast of troops of admirers, or of costly presents laid at her feet. The artists of modern times, in painting the scene in Simon's house at Bethany, have indeed adorned the grateful worshipper at Jesus' feet with surpassing beauty. But the sacred historian does not say that she was beautiful. We are left to infer the contrary, from the fact that she lived alone in the house with her brother and sister in a land where the lot of unmarried women was one of peculiar neglect.

She had no thought of doing anything just to make herself remembered, by anointing the feet of Jesus. She had not seen him in his glory. She did not know that even then legions of angels were ready to wait on their Lord. She saw in him one whom the world despised, and she must have known that the rulers of her people were bent upon putting him to death. And it was just because she, a timid and sensitive woman, braved the scorn of the world and the rebuke of friends in her own home, to declare her love for Jesus, that she obtained for herself an honorable and blessed memorial which shall outlast all time. It was by her self-forgetting devotion to one, whom others were impatient to destroy, that she gained for herself an everlasting name that shall not be cut off.

And so, evermore, Christ will keep the good name of all who count no sacrifice too costly to be offered upon the altar of faith and love to him. Their names shall be ever before him, graven upon the palms of his hands and precious in his sight. They shall be remembered with gratitude when the selfish are despised and the proud are put to shame. The grand aim and purpose of life is most sure to be gained by him who forgets everything but duty, is animated by nothing but love. To be happy ourselves, we must live to make others happy. To have all the good that riches can buy, we must give all we have to Christ.

The most wretched lot in the world may be his, who is furthest removed from the necessity to toil and to suffer. Better is it to pour out possessions, talents and affections in grateful devotion to Christ, and in that way seek for happiness here and glory hereafter, than to expend upon self everything that the world can give; and then go, to be told beyond the grave, "remember that thou in thy lifetime hadst thy good things."

Every day's observation proves that no advantage of birth, or condition, or talent, or success can procure happiness even in this life; no afflictions or losses can take away the true joy of living which comes from a good conscience and a heart at peace with God. In the splendid and coveted mansion of the millionaire, there are wounded hearts that no medicine of the physician can heal. In the gorgeously furnished apartments of princely homes, there are sighings and groanings of spirit to which no hired services can minister relief. You may recline at noonday upon couches where kings might repose amid splendors befitting their royal state; your bed at night may be canopied with purple and silken draperies wrought with all the costly and graceful devices of art, and yet in sleep you may find no rest, and in waking wish that life and consciousness had never come back.

In the gay and gorgeous hall at midnight, where artificial light outflames the sun, and voluptuous music intoxicates and maddens the passions of earth, may be seen the beautiful and bright-robed, radiant with smiles and floating like birds of paradise upon the mazes of the dance. And yet they may carry in their own bosoms, beneath the blaze of gems and the flash of sparkling eyes, the torture of fires that die not. To them, the soft strain that breathes in the lull of voices and the pause of mirth may seem like the wail of the pitying spirits of heaven over souls that are lost. Reposing at luxurious ease in the brilliant carriage which flashes along the street, and attracts the admiring gaze of all beholders, may be seen one who has come forth from an unhappy home at mid-day, calling it morning, striving to lose in the open air, the torturing burden of an hour, and yet returning disappointed, with the burden still on the heart, wearied without exertion and wretched without cause.

And yet such is the lot, to attain which, millions would sacrifice their souls. Such is the happiness of those who choose, and in judgment rather than in mercy, are permitted to have all their good things in this lifetime. And the opposite extreme of want and neglect, is just as full of envy and disappointment and despair to those who think happiness depends upon any earthly state, and who never learn to live by faith on the Son of

God. To that faith belongs the greatest victories ever gained in this world.

In his floorless cabin, weary, hungering and cold, the simple-hearted Christian bondman laid down to sleep in his crib of straw. He had toiled all his life long for another's gain, and he had no hope that he should ever be anything else in this world than the unpaid vassal of another's will. And yet the transforming faith of that poor slave, made his lowly cabin a holy place where angels delighted to go, on messages of love from the throne of heaven. Like the scourged and imprisoned apostles in the olden time, he woke at midnight to pray and sing praises unto Jesus. In his sleeping and in his waking hours, he dreamed and he sung of a kingdom that shall have no end and of a crown that he should wear when the fetters of bondage were broken. And that poor slave, with such lofty expectations, was richer and happier than all the wealth and glory of nations could make him without the hope of eternal life.

I have seen an aged Christian woman whose life for twenty years had been spent in darkness as deep as the blackest midnight. In all that time she had not been cheered in her desolation by the light of one human smile; she had not seen a flower blossom, nor a star shine, nor a single change come over the face of God's beautiful earth. Darkness had come upon the whole visible world to her, and had shut her in as with an impenetrable wall on every side, and her imprisoned spirit yearned in vain to find the lost day. And so she knew that she must live as long as life lasted, with no hope left save that her Bible, which she could no longer read, was still true, and that her Saviour, to whom she gave the love of her youthful heart long years before, would be with her in all her affliction. The grave itself could not be darker than the living tomb in which the soul was already buried. She must go at the summons of death without ever seeing the face of her own children, only hearing their voices bidding her farewell in the dark.

And yet that aged sufferer, with blindness added to many other afflictions, did not complain. The cloud that had veiled the bodily vision, did not cast a shadow upon the soul.

When I endeavored to commiserate her unhappy condition in the loss of sight, she said with the simplicity of a child's faith, "I shall soon see. The long night is almost gone, and I am looking for the dawn. When death opens the door, I shall pass from this dark prison into the full day." As I visited that aged disciple at different times in successive years, I always left her humble abode with the feeling that all the kingdoms of the earth, and the glory of them all, were a worthless bauble compared with the serene and quiet faith with which she leaned upon her Saviour's supporting hand, and pressed on under the heavy cloud of continual night, in the dark pilgrimage of life, without murmuring and without fear.

And I wish it were not so hard to make others believe the words, when I say that a calm and obedient trust in God is worth as much to the young, the healthful and the strong in their prosperity as it was to that blind and aged woman in her affliction. I would that all could be persuaded to walk in the light, before the darkness of trouble and sorrow comes, and the night of death settles down without any promise of returning day.

4. A GOOD WORK NEVER LOST.

The "good work," which Mary wrought upon Jesus at Bethany by anointing him for his burial is not the only one which shall live forever. The everlasting memorial of her simple faith, kept alive and tenderly cherished in a wicked world, is a promise that no act of duty shall ever be forgotten before God, or ever lose its power to do good. Jesus himself will remember and reward the simplest service, though it be but a cup of cold water given in his name. Every purpose and every effort of right-doing shall have its record in the book of life, and its influence shall be kept alive to guide and to bless, to instruct and to save, long as the world shall stand.

The light of Christian example and Christian instruction may be diminished and obstructed by the cloud of ignorance and unbelief, but it is light still, and it can never be put out. Evil has indeed thus far prevailed over good to a fearful extent in this world, but it is not the strongest power, it shall not always conquer, it shall not live forever. Good by its very nature is immortal. God will no more suffer it to die than he will forget the work of his own hands or forsake the soul that cries to him for help. The humblest and poorest of the disciples of Jesus can start waves of blessing that shall deepen and widen and flow forever. You need not know, you need not suspect that you are doing anything great; you need not weary yourself with busy anxieties about success. You have only to go on quietly, faithfully, doing the work which God's providence assigns you, and you may be sure that the memorial of your life will be written in the book of heaven, and there will be redeemed souls in the final day to call you blessed.

The silent, teachable, trusting look with which Mary watched the countenance and caught the words of Jesus is still preaching to millions. The world is indeed full of hurry, of violence and of conflict, and it may seem to us a waste of breath to speak gentle words in the face of the whirlwind of strife. And yet in such a world God has promised that his gentleness shall make his people great; by suffering they shall grow strong; by failure they shall learn success, and by defeat they shall conquer.

The calmness and the self-possession of a right purpose and a pure heart disarm opposition and win more than violence. The rudest nature, that would hurl back threatening and rebuke with fiercer words of wrath, may be mastered and melted into penitence and love by a single look like that which Jesus turned upon Peter. You need not wait for great occasions, you need not ask for extraordinary abilities, you need not have a thought what the world will think of you; only let your daily walk be a living testimony unto Jesus, and God will keep that testimony in the world, widening and deepening and intensifying in power, long as the Gospel shall be preached for the salvation of men.

Every world in the material universe is bound to every other by immutable law, and no atom is ever lost from the immensity of things created. The circlet of waves produced by the fall of a pebble travels to the uttermost parts of the sea. The blow that I strike with my hand is felt around the earth and beyond the stars. Much more pervasive and enduring are those moral influences that form the character and fix the destiny of immortal beings. Every act of duty starts a wave of light and of blessing that shall roll and expand for endless ages. It is the sceptic's dismal philosophy which says, "The good that men do in their lives is interred with their bones." In the service of Christ effort is success and a right purpose is victory, and no faithful laborer can fail to find many among the host of the redeemed to call him blessed.

Not many years ago, a European philosopher, unrolling the countless bandages of an Egyptian mummy, found a few grains of wheat in the black and withered hand. Curiosity led him to plant the kernels in the colder soil of the north. The germ of life which had been imprisoned three thousand years in the dark charnel of death, responded to the touch of warmth and moisture and light, and shot forth the green stalk and matured the ripened grain. And now, year by year, broad fields sown from the produce of those revived kernels of Egyptian wheat wave their rich harvests beneath the autumnal sun, and thousands of lives are sustained by food, the fruitful germ of which was so long imprisoned in the house of death.

And so the laborer in any department of Christian service, by precept or by example, may drop the seed-corn of the divine word into the cold, dead heart of the world, and many seasons may pass, and he may see no signs that the seed sown in patience and in sorrow will ever germinate or even retain its life. He may go on year after year, faithful though despondent and sad of heart, making ten thousand unrecognized, unapplauded efforts for the good of others, and at last he may go down to the grave, feeling that nothing of all that he has done will live after him to bless the world or to cause his name to be remembered with gratitude.

And yet the countless years of heaven alone may be sufficient to estimate the blessed fruit springing from that life of toil, of patience and of disappointment. It may yet be found that the most needed and successful laborers in God's great vineyard of the world were they who were willing to toil on without apparent or applauded success, but simply because they believed that no right purpose, no well-meant effort could ever fail of its appropriate result or be forgotten before God. The great contest which truth is waging for the mastery of this world continues through all the ages, and the delay of a year or of a century is no indication that truth has lost its power, or that the divine purpose is defeated.

Two hundred years ago, John Flavel, of Dartmouth, in England, driven out of his pulpit by the persecuting Act of Uniformity, was preaching in an open field. With his wonted earnestness and affectionate fervor of address, he spoke of the dreadful curse resting on all who love not the Lord Jesus Christ. Among the listeners on that day was a youth of fifteen, who heard the solemn words of the preacher, and went away as though he heard them not. Some of noble birth and of high intellectual culture were so deeply affected that they fell senseless upon the ground. But that thoughtless young man only listened and looked on as if he were a disinterested spectator. Soon afterwards he began a roving life upon the seas, and finally settled down for a permanent home, a faithless and a prayerless man, in America. Meanwhile, Flavel continued to preach the gospel which he loved, amid persecutions and many sorrows, and when the last joyful summons came, he went home to God in peace.

And eighty-five years passed by, from that day of field-preaching at Dartmouth, and the boy of fifteen was now a man of a hundred years and still a wanderer from God. The quick susceptibilities of youth had died in his old and guilty heart long ago. No ordinary faith could have believed that the seed-corn of divine truth planted by John Flavel's preaching eighty-five years before, on the other side of the ocean, still survived and was destined to spring up and bear fruit unto life eternal. But so it was. It chanced on a certain day that he found himself alone in an open field belonging to his own farm, with no weeping multitude around him to awaken his sympathies, and no preacher's solemn voice to tell him of his sin. Moved, he knew not how, that old man, in his hundredth year, passing over all the intervening space of time felt himself back again in the field at Dartmouth, hearing the fearful words, "If any man love not the Lord Jesus Christ, let him be accursed." And the message of heaven, which the thoughtless youth so easily rejected, was mightier when speaking from the remembered past than when heard from the living voice. Then first the aged sinner found strength to roll the burden of the threatened curse from his heart, through the exercise of penitent and trusting love. He lived to the extraordinary age of a hundred and sixteen years, believing and rejoicing in the Saviour, whom, for a century, he had rejected. And the awakening call of duty, which roused him from the sleep of impenitence and unbelief, came from the remembered words of one who had rested from his labor for more than half a century.

Such is the persistency with which the truth retains its life and germinating power, even when sown in the uncongenial soil of the depraved heart. And one such example of effort apparently lost, living and working for good long after the laborer himself has forgotten his work, may give us hope and encouragement as we sow the seed of life beside all waters, morning, evening and at noon of day, withholding not our hand.

5. THE COMMON LOT.

If a home on earth could be free from the anxiety, the suspense and the silent anguish of waiting on the sick and the dying, it would seem that it should be the home where Jesus so often sought refuge from the cold and contentious world, and ever found sympathizing friends and a welcome hospitality. If any family on earth could be justified in feeling themselves secure for a time against the dreaded visitation of death, it must be the one towards which Jesus was drawn by ties of the deepest and most constant love.

And yet the great woe inflicted upon the whole human race by transgression is too deep and dreadful to spare even them. The one, all-pitiless destroyer, that was never yet restrained from his work by the revered aspect of age, or the wail of helpless infancy, or any degree of loveliness in human character, must not spare even the home where the Son of God in the last days of his ministry found his only rest. There, where the Comforter of all sorrows, the Healer of all diseases, the Giver of all life, so often went to repose after the weary day spent in the narrow and noisy streets of Jerusalem—there came the dread shadow of sore affliction, and darkened the light of the window, and sat down unbidden at the daily board, and lingered in the quiet chamber, and would not be persuaded to depart, day nor night. In the very house where Jesus had so many times sat at meat and cheered all hearts with words and looks of love, in the very chamber where he had slept at night and from which he had gone forth in the morning, leaving the blessing of peace behind him, there must be the silent step which waits upon the suffering, the sympathizing look which strives in vain to conceal anxiety, and the suppressed voice which whispers hope, while the heart is heavy with fear. The very one upon whom the family must be most dependent for the preservation of its name, and for support in the time of trial and adversity, is smitten down by relentless disease.

The alarmed and sorrowing sisters watch by night and by day the growing symptoms of a fatal result, and they exhaust every remedy in the vain effort to sustain the sinking powers of life. It now seems to avail them nothing that Jesus was their friend, and that he had often shared the hospitality of the family, and had given them many tokens of affectionate regard for the suffering and dying brother. They are in trouble, and are anxiously looking for any sign of hope or relief; but they find none, and their divine Friend is far away beyond Jordan, and it might cost him his life if he should come to help them. The quiet home towards which Jesus had so many times bent his footsteps at evening and where his presence had filled every heart with peace must soon be made dark with mourning and death.

And such is still the lot of the families which Jesus loves in all the earth. There are many such, and he has long been with them in spirit, a frequent and a familiar guest. At evening-tide, in the night watches, and when the morning brings the gladness of the new day, they welcome Jesus to their homes and to their hearts. They set before him the best of all they have, and they only wish they could give him more, and that he would make his abode with them. In him, they see the brightness of the eternal Father's glory brought so near, and clothed with so much of human kindness, that they reverently call him Brother, and trust in him as the support and guardian of the household.

And yet affliction will not be forbidden to smite such families. Death will not be commanded to spare the parent, the brother, the sister or the child whom Jesus loves. The very Friend in whom they most confide, who is himself most deeply interested in their welfare, and who can do all things for them in the hour of need, will not command the destroyer, in his goings forth through this sorrow-stricken world, to pass by their dwelling without entering. Infinitely gracious and compassionate as Jesus is, he does not promise to turn aside the stroke of affliction, even from those who walk most closely with him in the journey of life. He is willing to visit the most wretched home and watch with the suffering in the darkest hour, but his presence will not dismiss all pain. Even to his dearest friends he still says, "In this world ye shall have tribulation." When they ask for a home where there shall be no more sorrow, he points to the gateway of death.

And, besides, the great sympathizing High Priest of our profession has taught us, by his own example, how great and godlike it is to suffer and to be made perfect by suffering. The serene and blessed heights of peace and joy are attained by those who have climbed the rugged steeps of pain and toil. God sends the sorest chastisement upon his most beloved children, that they may be made white in the furnace of affliction, and be presented without spot before his throne. The troubles and disquietudes of this earthly life will prove ministers of mercy, if they make us cling to our Father's hand, and long for rest in our Father's house. The single eye of faith can see the bow of promise upon the darkest cloud. The quick ear of obedience and affection can hear the voice of love amid the thunders of the wildest storm.

We do not know when, or under what circumstances, the journey of our life will close, but it need not be in darkness or despair. Some will be called without a moment's warning; some will be led down to the grave slowly, through months and years of weariness and pain; some will be called when life is most dear, and all its pursuits and pleasures charm them most; and some will stay long after trouble and disappointment have made it a weariness to live. The youngest of a family may be taken first. The strongest and most healthful may be struck down, while the feeble must wait on them in their prostration and mourn for them when they are gone. One who has been waiting and expecting to go any day for years, may at last be taken by surprise. One may be called when his plans for worldly business are mature, and in the most successful operation; another when all his earthly affairs are unsettled, and no one can fill his place, and his removal will cause the greatest embarrassment to his dearest friends; another must go to the house appointed for all the living, just as he has completed every arrangement to spend his declining years in retirement and peace. One may toil for years in patience and poverty and disappointment, and when at last the hour of success comes, he must leave it for others to enjoy; another may have little of struggle or conflict, less of failure or disappointment, and yet he too just as certainly must die.

Such are the inevitable conditions of this earthly life. The gospel tells the affecting story of affliction and death coming upon the family that Jesus most tenderly loved, as if to assure us, in the most touching manner, that it is the portion, even of the accepted children of God, in this world to suffer and to die. There is nothing left for us to do, if we would be wise, but to conform our earthly plans to the common lot, and to cherish hopes for the endless future, such as affliction and death cannot destroy.

6. THE MESSAGE.

When the fatal sickness fell upon Lazarus at Bethany, his alarmed and afflicted sisters sent and told Jesus. They were in trouble, and they had reason to fear the worst, but it was a calm and confiding message that they sent. "Lord, behold he whom thou lovest is sick.". The bearer of the heavy tidings must make his way down the steep and rocky path to Jericho, and across the Jordan, to the desert place where Jesus had retired with his disciples. The going and returning must be a journey of days. And yet there is no sign of hurry or impatience in the message which the sisters sent. They safely presumed that the love of Jesus for their dying brother, would prompt him to do all that their own love could desire to have done. It was enough for them that Jesus should know that Lazarus was sick.

I remember well myself to have been sent, when a child, as the bearer of heavy tidings to a family living some miles distant. And I was instructed only to say to an afflicted sister, that

her brother was dead. In that case too it was taken for granted, that a sincere affection for the afflicted family would dictate whatever were best to be done. I was not told to ask the friends at a distance to come to those upon whom the heavy stroke had fallen, but only to say that death had entered the household. It was not for a moment supposed that such a message could be received with indifference.

Such confidence had the afflicted sisters at Bethany, in the warmth and sincerity of Christ's love for them, and for their dying brother. And it was therefore the most natural thing in the world that they should send so brief and simple a message to him, when they were so greatly afflicted: "Behold, he whom thou lovest is sick."

Our risen and glorified Lord is as worthy of our confidence, now that he sits upon the throne of heaven, as he was when he came a homeless wanderer, to be entertained at the friendly house in Bethany. And our faith in the reality of his love should not fail us, when sickness darkens the light of our homes, and death enters the household. First of all in the day of our affliction, we should fly upon the swift wings of prayer to tell the tidings of our trouble unto Jesus. Nothing that touches our hearts with joy or grief, is too trifling to be told to him. The greatest sorrow shall be easily borne with such help as he can give. Our greatest Friend will have a right to feel himself wronged, if we pour out our grief to others, and shut our hearts to him.

For the great sorrows of life, there is little alleviation, there is no absolute cure, save that which the coming of Jesus brings to the weary heart. If we seek the help of Jesus first, we shall spare ourselves much disappointment in looking to others for consolation. When those, who have exhausted every other resource in vain, are constrained at last to look to Jesus for rest, they are filled with surprise and joy, to find that the best and greatest Friend, was all the while knocking at the door and waiting to be admitted.

The little child runs to the mother with the tale of every joy and every sorrow. And when we become like children in faith, and so are fitted for the kingdom of heaven, we shall as naturally go to our Father with all our griefs and all our joys. The cares and toils of which we speak to our human friends, will still be named with open and reverent hearts, when we come to our Father in prayer. It is due to our best Friend that we shall never doubt the reality of his love. He does not need to be importuned into an interest in our welfare. The very trial that tasks our faith most severely, and makes it seem to us that he has forsaken us, has been sent in mercy to give us more peace and confidence in him when the trial is past. The whole earthly life of Jesus is an infinite demonstration of the depth of his love for the helpless and the unworthy. Against all the suggestions of unbelief, against all the discouragements that arise from new discoveries of our need, we have this one assurance,— "While we were yet sinners, Christ died for us." Surely we cannot come to such a Friend too often, we cannot speak too plainly or too confidingly to him, of anything that gives us grief or trouble or joy.

7. THE SUSPENSE.

When the message came from the sisters at Bethany to Jesus at Bethabara, he replied immediately,—"This sickness is not unto death." The messenger returned with joy, hurrying along the steep and stony track of the mountain road, impatient to relieve the anxious household with the glad intelligence that the beloved brother should not die. What must have been his surprise and confusion, on reaching the house, to find that Lazarus was already in his grave. How much it would add to the grief and perplexity of the bereaved sisters when he should tell them what Jesus had said. How sorely would it task their confidence in the truth, the wisdom, and the love of their greatest and best Friend, to have word brought from him, that their brother should not die, on the very evening of the day when they had followed the cold and lifeless body to the tomb.

"Had Jesus sent that word in mistaken kindness to keep their hearts from despondency, while as yet himself did not know what the end would be? Was he experimenting with the power of hope to sustain the suffering and to shake off the grasp of disease? Had Jesus promised what he could not perform? Had his great power forsaken him, and must those who had looked to him for miraculous aid, at last confess that he had become as weak as they? Had he given the positive assurance of recovery to his dearest friend, the very day that others had carried that friend in sorrow to the grave? Had Jesus designedly staid in distant Bethabara to save himself from witnessing a scene of suffering which he could not relieve? Had he refused to come back with the messenger, that he might avoid the distrust and reproaches of those who once confided in his power to heal all manner of disease?"

Such doubts and fears must have tried the hearts of the afflicted sisters of Bethany, during the four dark days of mourning, more severely than the actual death of their brother. They had always known that Lazarus and themselves also must sooner or later die, but they had hoped that the word of Jesus would never fail. If he had only staid where he was, after receiving tidings of their affliction, they could have understood that; for they knew that it would be at the peril of his life, if he came to them. But how must it have wrung their hearts with anguish, to think of their brother sleeping in the cold tomb, and at the same time of the strange and apparently mistaken word of Jesus, "This sickness is not unto death."

So is it with us all in the dark days of affliction and despondency. The cloud casts its thick shadows all around us; our hopes fail; our hearts are weary, and life is a burden. But if we walk trustingly on in the darkness, till we learn the great lesson of faith, Jesus himself will take us by the hand and lead us forth to the light, and we shall see his face in a broader and brighter day. In the review of the past we shall learn that our infinite Helper was by our side and bending over us with unutterable love when we were prostrate and thought ourselves utterly forsaken. We never see him as he sees us. We are never as ready to receive his help, as he is to relieve our need. We have attained the highest joy of life when we have learned to take what God.

gives with a grateful heart, and to live for his glory equally in sickness and in health, in abundance and in want. The Son of God is glorified, the word of peace is preached to the world, by all who suffer with Christ in patience and in hope. The days and nights of weariness and pain are precious to those who walk the fiery furnace of affliction in company with the Son of man.

8. THE RELIEF.

Two days after the sad news came from Bethany, Jesus told the disciples what had befallen the family of his friend, and proposed to go and comfort them in their affliction. He would not delay too long, lest the trial of their faith might end in unbelief and despair. He would not go too soon, lest he should deprive them of the best opportunity to behold his glory in his power over death. However perilous it might be to his own life, he would not refuse to go at the call of those who had received him at their own house, and afforded him a quiet and safe retreat from the contentious and cavilling world.

To al. who have welcomed him to their homes and their hearts, in the days of health and prosperity, he will come with the blessing of peace and consolation, when sorrow darkens around them, and death enters the household. He comes to all even now in meekness and in lowliness, willing to dwell in the humblest home, able to cheer the saddest heart. He stands long at many a door, waiting for admission. He suffers the indignity of delay and rejection, only that he may win his way to the heart by kindness and be received as a friend.

It may be easy for many to reject him in the day of their pride and prosperity. But even the prayerless and the profane will call for the ministers and disciples of Jesus when the hand of death is upon them. How much better it were for them to receive Jesus himself as a constant and familiar friend when the heart is glad and the cup of earthly blessing runs over, and then he will not be far from them in the hour of their greatest need.

9. TWELVE HOURS IN THE DAY.

Jesus goes in good time, to explain and fulfill.

his assurance that the sickness of Lazarus should not be unto death. His disciples feared that the journey might be attended with danger to him and to themselves, and they accordingly endeavored to dissuade him from making the attempt. Jesus silenced their remonstrances by declaring that every man has his work assigned, and that while he walks in the light of truth, no power on earth can prevent the accomplishment of all that God has given him to do.

We shall all have time enough to do our work well, if we improve the hours as they are given; and when our task is done, there will be time enough to rest. Life is never too short to them who live for God. There is no such thing as loss or failure, to them who seek infinite riches in the love of Christ. Those that walk with Jesus, can tread the roughest path of life with firm and even step, without haste, without rest, doing the duty which the day brings, and ready for the morrow when the morrow comes. The hurry and the waste, the fear of failure and the hope of success, upon which millions weary their hearts, all come from neglecting the proper work of life, or attempting to do what had better never be done. Invincible energy is treasured up in the repose of a good conscience; unquenchable zeal lives and burns beneath the calm of a spirit that communes with Jesus.

A great Christian statesman and scholar adopted this rule for the division of time;— "Give eight hours of the twenty-four to toil, eight to devotion and recreation, eight to rest, and all to God." It is the giving of all to God, that makes every day profitable, and saves the loss of a single hour. If we make it our great study to live in harmony with God's providence, and in obedience to his word, we shall have time and talents and opportunity to do all our work and to do it well.

However many months and years of life men may throw away, however much they may burden themselves with cares and business, and plead worldly engagements for the neglect of duty, God will give all a time for one great and solemn work, and when the hour comes, all other engagements will have to give place to that. God will give all a time to die. God gives opportunities for repentance and faith, for prayer and for the study of his word, for doing good to others, and for all Christian work; and men may use the opportunity for a thousand other things, rather than the one which God chooses. But there is one call which none can defer, none can deny.

A hard driven slave of mammon toiled all the week, and found the days too few to finish all that his greedy soul desired to do. The blessed Sabbath morning found him back at his desk, with bills and ledgers around him, too busy to keep the holy day. Half of the afternoon was gone before he could find time to rest. All Monday, he laughed within at the cunning cheat, by which he had stolen time from God, and got the start of the world for a week. Tuesday morning tidings came to his breakfast-table, that death had entered the house of a neighbor and friend, the previous night. "Ah! indeed, but it is very different with me. I am so busy I could not find time to die." The fool's jest was still on his lip, when he rose, walked, fell upon the floor. His hour had come. He had pressing work, and many things that nobody but himself could do that day. But he was not too busy to die.

"There are twelve hours in the day." There is a fixed and appointed season of duty, of toil and of blessing, for all in this world. While that season lasts, God's favor will shine upon your path and make it all light. Improve the season well, and so when nothing more remains for you to do, to enjoy or to suffer here, be ready to pass in peace, through the rest and sleep of death, into the endless and blessed life.

10. THE BLESSED SLEEP.

Death is the most awful thunderbolt of the divine wrath that has ever fallen upon this earth. In all the languages of men, in all ages of human history, it has been named the king of terrors. From him who is living without God in the world, it cuts off every hope, it destroys every possession, it blasts every joy. To him, beauty of form, and pride of place, and glory of intellect are but dust and ashes when death comes to change his face and send him away. Let philosophy arm itself with studied and proud resolution; let worldliness march blindly on, refusing to think of anything beyond this life; let romance strew the grave with flowers, and art make the habitations of the dead more beautiful than the homes of the living; and still death, in any form, under any circumstances, is awful.

In no way does Jesus assume a more complete superiority over everything that we have to fear, than by taking away the terror of death. To those who believe in him he makes death only a sleep, a peaceful and holy rest, the awakening from which shall be the beginning of a new and a blessed life.

Toil is the best preparation for rest. The sleep of the laboring man is sweet. No medicine of the physician, no exemption from care, no luxuries of house, or service, or table, can command such refreshing sleep as honest labor brings to the weary every night. And so the sleep of death will be sweet and welcome to all whose work of life is done. Life is the time for toil. It is the fool that says to his soul, "Take thine ease." The call for more laborers in every part of God's great vineyard, grows louder and louder as new fields of usefulness are opened, and the facilities for doing good are multiplied. In such a time, none but a recreant and an idler would make it his study to shun responsibility and seek repose.

There is no promise that assured rest will be given here, and those who fix their hearts upon attaining it, are sure to be disappointed. There are many who work hard and wear out all their strength, to lay up for themselves a few years of rest on earth, and yet never find an hour of calm and abundant peace. They toil and weary themselves, like galley slaves, in the hard service of the world, and then, when all is done, are compelled to make the bitter confession that they have spent their strength for naught. The work and the weariness of life have been theirs in full measure, and yet they have never been encouraged and comforted by the assurance that when the toil of life is done, they shall sleep in Jesus and find rest. They bind themselves with heavy bonds to the god of this world; they consent to be made slaves and bow down beneath heavy burdens; they give their hearts to be pierced and tortured with care and anxiety; they deny themselves the true joy of living and get nothing for their pains but regret and disappointment. When the Master comes to take account of their work, they have nothing to show but misimproved talents and wasted hours. They must go down to the grave with no hope that the sleep of death will bring them to the morn of a blessed and an endless life.

But to the faithful laborer, who has toiled and suffered to the end, in loving devotion to his heavenly King, Jesus himself will come in good time to awake him out of sleep, and to clothe him in the robes of immortality. He shall hear the voice which the dead Lazarus heard in Bethany, and shall come forth to a new life whose serene and tireless activity shall be the truest rest for the soul.

11. THE MERCIFUL ABSENCE.

The inability of infinite love to cease from loving and helping the unworthy, is one of the wonders of revelation. When Jesus told his disciples plainly that Lazarus was dead, he said, " I am glad for your sakes, that I was not there, to the intent that ye may believe." He ventured to be thought for a time unkind and forgetful of his friend, that he might show the greater kindness in the end. If he had been at Bethany, and had seen the progress of the disease under which Lazarus was hastening to the grave, compassion for the suffering one and for his alarmed and afflicted relatives, would have constrained him to put forth his miraculous power and arrest the disease, and so he would have deprived himself of the opportunity to perform the greater miracle of raising the dead. He confesses himself unable to witness the sorrow of his friends, in the house of sickness and death, without putting forth his divine power for their relief; and that too when he had the strongest reasons for withholding his hand for a while, that he might do the greater work in the end.

And such is still his compassion for the suffering and the needy who trust in him. He cannot refrain himself from helping them. The same Jehovah-Jesus, the Angel of the Covenant, said unto Lot, "I cannot do anything till thou be come" to a place of safety.

Jacob discovered the unconquerable Angel, in the mysterious antagonist, against whom he had wrestled in the dark till the morning, and then he was not rebuked for saying, "I will not let thee go, except thou bless me." The lonely and defenseless man of Penuel, who feared that he should be destroyed by his angry brother Esau, had power with the infinite One by his very weakness, and prevailed.

The feebleness of the child overcomes the strong man's heart. So the Almighty Father cries in compassion over his erring and helpless children, "How shall I give thee up? Mine heart is turned within me, my repentings are kindled together." Ages before the Son of God appeared in fashion as a man, and by his meek and gentle spirit showed the true character of the Father to men, it was written, "Like as a father pitieth his children, so the Lord pitieth them that fear him. For he knoweth our frame, he remembereth that we are dust."

This is the great lesson which we all have to learn, through living faith in Christ the Son of God. Reason and nature can teach us much concerning a supreme, eternal and Almighty Creator. The gospel alone, with its human tenderness and touching simplicity, can make us acquainted with a paternal and pitying God. Inspiration alone may venture to say that human weakness can prevail over infinite power.

Multitudes pass through the world, restless, impatient, unhappy, all the way, always grasping at something beyond their reach; always dissatisfied with that which has cost them the most pains; always feeling that something for which they are not responsible stands in the way of their happiness. It would make life and the world all new to such, if they could only believe that they have a Father in heaven rich enough to bestow every blessing upon his children, and too kind to let them suffer except for their good. It would be the most glorious revelation to all the unhappy if they could see and believe that God cannot restrain himself from helping those who trust in him.

And these words are not simply for those who are already in trouble. It often does very little good to speak of God's pity to the afflicted, just because they have not learned to recognize his kindness in the day of prosperity. They then forgot that all blessing came from their heavenly Father, and they find it still harder to see, when the cloud is upon them, that affliction itself may be sent by him in still greater mercy. If we walk with God in the day of peace and prosperity, we shall find it easy to believe that he is still with us in the night of conflict and sorrow.

12. BE STILL.

When death entered the house of a Hebrew family, it was the signal for violent outcries and loud lamentations. The afflicted rent their garments, disfigured their faces, plucked out their hair, covered themselves with sackcloth and ashes and sat upon the ground. For many days, all the ordinary pursuits of life were given up; their only food was bread of affliction mingled with their own tears, and, to all outward appearance, they surrendered themselves to utter wretchedness and despair. In many cases hired mourners were employed to lift up their voices in weeping and wailing;

and sympathizing friends were ambitious to outdo each other in noisy demonstrations of woe, and thus in every way to increase the misery of those who mourned from real sorrow of heart. The custom often degenerated into a tiresome and unmeaning form, and the afflicted were wearied and oppressed, rather than comforted, by the ambitious and noisy condolence of their friends.

Such was the scene of mourning in the stricken house at Bethany, when the divine Comforter came, the fourth day after Lazarus had been carried to the grave. Many a time had friendly messengers gone down to the opening of the glen towards the east, and watched the companies of travelers climbing up the steep ascent of the mountain-path from Jericho, hoping that Jesus might be among them. Many a time had the bereaved sisters gone up to the housetop, and looked through their tears down the stony wilderness of Judea, and across the Jordan valley towards the distant Bethabara, while every sigh of their stricken hearts said, "Oh! that Jesus would come." Again and again had they questioned the messenger who came back from Jesus with the promise of recovery, if by any means they could learn the meaning of that strange word.

At last Jesus himself comes to explain and confirm his own message. But the blessed Comforter, who brings peace to troubled hearts will not go at once to the house where excited friends and guests are all gathered in one room, and everything is filled with the outcry and ceremony of woe. If he is to do anything for those who are truly afflicted, he must first see them apart from their vain and noisy comforters. He stops in a quiet place by the roadside, beneath the shoulder of the hill, while one of his company goes up into the town to tell the afflicted sisters where the Master may be found. One after the other they hurry to the spot and give utterance to the first gush of anguish at the feet of Jesus in the same words, "Lord, if thou hadst been here, my brother had not died." Then in that quiet spot before a crowd had gathered or it was generally known through the village that Jesus had come, he comforts the heart-broken sisters with his calm instructive and kindly words.

So on another occasion, when Jesus came by urgent request to a house which had just been visited by death, and he found the friends of the family filling the rooms, and the people making a noise with their outcries and lamentations, he would do nothing until the excited company were put forth and the afflicted ones, who needed his consolation, were able to give quiet and thoughtful attention to his words.

If ever it becomes us to be still, and know that the Lord is God, and to give patient and earnest attention to the voice of his holy providence, it is when he comes near us by the awful visitation of death. It is a very sacred and solemn season to the whole family, when one of their number lies dead in the house. God is there, speaking to them from the marble face and the silent lips which were so lately full of life. It should be their chief concern to understand and improve the lesson which the great preacher, death, is sent to teach. God has a gracious meaning and purpose, in his most afflictive dispensations, for the instruction of his children, and they should never let the world come in, with its forms and fashions, to divert their attention from their Father's voice. The world is proud and pretentious even in its grief. It would set up its exacting claims, and enforce its capricious laws, and dictate the garb and expression of sorrow in the midst of the family, when a voice speaks to them from the bed of death, and the open grave and the disclosed realities of judgment and eternity.

Let those, who believe in Jesus, behave themselves under affliction, as if he himself had come to the house, and had sat down quietly by their side to comfort them, and to teach them the great lesson of submission and faith. We need not be afraid to pour out all our sorrows before him, for he himself is touched with the feeling of our infirmities. In the days of his flesh, he expressed the anguish of his own heart with strong crying and many tears. When he saw others weeping around him at Bethany, he himself wept and groaned in spirit and was troubled. To such a Friend we may surely tell all our grief. But if we would receive such consolation as he alone can give, we must not let the world come in and weary our hearts with its studied form, and parade, and drapery of woe.

13. VAIN REGRET.

"Lord, if thou hadst been here, my brother had not died." The heart-stricken mourners of Bethany had faith enough in Jesus to believe that his presence with them, at an earlier day, could have saved them from their great affliction. They did not dare to believe that he had come to make what they most regretted the occasion of their deepest and most unutterable joy.

Too soon! too late! Alas! how often the words fall upon the ear like the clods of the grave upon the coffin. "Too soon," mourns the mother's bleeding heart when the pale shadow of death settles down upon the cherub brow of her innocent babe. "Too soon," answers the light-hearted youth, when Jesus comes with infinite love in every look, and says, "Give me thy heart, follow me." "Too soon," sighs the weary and disappointed worldling, when pleasure loses its charm and desire fails, and the shadows of age, and disease, and death gather around his path.

"Too late," moans the stricken parent, when told that a wiser physician, or better remedies would have saved the life of a beloved child. "Too late," whispers the fainting invalid, who has sought a more genial clime for recovery when disease has already poisoned the fountains of life. "Too late," sighs the dying sinner, who is told upon the bed of death that the voice of mercy still pleads for him.

And so, with multitudes, the memory of the past is strewn all the way with bitter regret. If only something different had been done, from what has been done, then they suppose the present would be all peace and the future all hope. So they fondly dream, not considering that what they most regret in the past may have been sent in mercy, or may yet be improved so as to be the occasion of endless joy in the future. It is not for us to suppose that our divine Deliverer has lost his interest in our welfare because we cannot see his face in the dark hour of trial and temptation.

The night was black with clouds and tempest

upon the sea of Galilee, and a little bark, that bore the teachers and reformers of the world, was struggling with the waves and in danger of perishing. The disciples believed that if Jesus were with them on board, his presence might save them in the extremity of their danger. They had no thought that his eye could see them through the darkness from the distant shore, or that he could come to them walking upon the waves. They could only regret that they had put out to sea on such a night, and that Jesus was left alone on the land. But when he came, and the storm was hushed, and the ship was safe at the shore whither they went, their regret was changed into joy. Then the hard rowing against the wind, and the violence of the waves, and the blackness of the storm, and the imminence of the danger were remembered with gratitude as the means of bringing forth the power and glory of their Master in brighter display.

And such would be the happy result of every trial and temptation to which we are exposed, if we could only have faith enough to toil on, and hope on, till the hour of success and deliverance comes. It is not necessary for us to see the hand that guards our way. We have only to press on in the course of duty at God's command, and if at times it seems to us that we must step upon the void, we shall find the rock beneath.

When disaster and disappointment have befallen us, and our wisest plans and noblest purposes are defeated, it does not become us to mourn and despair, as if all were lost. We must all find much in the past to regret. And he often sees most to regret, who has been most in earnest to improve his time well. But it is by mistakes and failures that the conscientious learn, and the diligent improve. Defeat in a single battle is often the condition of success in the whole campaign. The apparent withholding of the divine blessing for a season, prepares for a more abundant harvest in the end.

The reapers find two kinds of wheat in the field in the time of harvest. One grew from seed sown in the early spring. The warm sun, and frequent showers, and mellow earth, caused it to shoot up a rapid growth, and to bring forth its mature and ripened grain, without any appearance of delay or failure. The other was sown when the heat of summer was already past, and the falling dews were changed to frost, and the snows of winter were close at hand. It had scarcely become rooted in the soil before the earth was firmly locked in fetters of ice, the process of growth was arrested, and, for successive months, the whole vegetable world was wrapped in the pall of death. But when the warm spring breathed upon the earth again, the winter grain was prepared to shoot up the more vigorously, because the severity of frost and snow had compelled it to take deeper root in the earth. And the harvest is ever most abundant from the grain that has been checked in its first growth, cropped down and trampled upon by grazing flocks, and buried beneath drifted snow.

So does God send the long, cold winter of trial and delay and disappointment, to give his people time to deepen and enlarge the foundations of their faith. Then when the heavens are opened, and the gracious rain descends, the seed of the divine word, which has been sown in patience and sorrow, springs up and brings forth the most abundant harvest.

14. THE RESURRECTION AND THE LIFE.

"I am the resurrection and the life." These are the words of a King and a Conqueror—a King to reign over all the gifts and joys of life, a Conqueror to subdue all the fear and power of death. Standing by the grave of one whom he deeply loved, surrounded by weeping mourners, himself soon to expire upon the cross, Jesus claims the keys of death. He assumes the right and the power to give eternal life to whom he will. He stands forth, in his living person, the sole and divine champion for the defense and deliverance of the human race; for the arrest of that destruction which has burdened all languages with sounds of woe, and made the earth one universal grave. He is not simply a prophet who comes into the world upon a mission of instruction. He is himself the truth, which he proclaims. He is the life, which he offers to the world. He is able to destroy death, and to clothe this mortal with immortality.

These words which Jesus spoke by the roadside as he drew near to Bethany, have already gone out with light and blessing to the ends of the earth. Ten thousand thousand times have these words brought peace and hope to troubled hearts, in the darkened chamber of suffering, in the hush of the house of mourning, in the still presence of the dead, and beside the open grave. Faith has graven the blessed words upon the tomb to proclaim its triumph over the king of terrors. The great host of the redeemed from all lands, from all times, passing on in continued procession to the heavenly Zion, have marched through the gates of death to the same song.

Oh! ye sons and daughters of affliction, who go to weep at the grave of your beloved, and refuse to be comforted because they come not back; ye fearful and unbelieving, who dread the approach of the last bitter hour, and cannot bear to think of closing your eyes forever upon all this living world; ye disappointed and murmuring, whose earthly hopes are all buried in the deep grave of the past, and whose daily experience is only a renewal of murmuring and disappointment; hear the words of Jesus, "I am the resurrection and the life." Not all the harps of heaven could breathe such peace into the troubled soul as all may attain through faith in the meaning and mighty power of these words. Take them to your hearts. Learn by experience what words can never teach. Gain the victory over all your sorrows, fears and disappointments by trusting in him who alone has eternal life to give.

The most cherished expectations of earthly good may be utterly cut off. The temporal possessions which have been guarded with every possible security, may take wings and fly away. He who labors hardest in the beaten track of this earthly life, may find the least reward. The rich and the poor, the old and the young, the healthful and the diseased, the honored and the despised will all die. No one can tell in what direction his sorest disappointment will come. No prophet of the Lord will be sent to prepare the way before the messenger of death.

And yet the word of Jesus can never fail, "He

that believeth in me shall never die." The hopes upon which he most relies shall ever live. The sources from which he derives the deepest joy shall never fail. His most precious treasures shall be ever increasing in value. For his greatest wants he shall be ever finding a more certain and full supply. The objects of desire on which he fixes his heart most intently, shall grow in value the more severely he tests their worth. The most cherished attachments which he forms in the journey of life, shall be renewed and confirmed forever in a better land. One infinite Friend who can command and bestow all possible blessing shall always be ready to do for him exceeding abundantly, above all that he can ask or think. The grave shall be to him the gateway of life, and through its dark portals he shall pass into the land of endless light.

Surely of such an one it is safe to say, " He shall never die." He shall never lose the joy, the glory, the blessedness of that life whose ever-flowing fountain is faith in the Son of God.

15. JESUS WEPT.

Xerxes wept when he surveyed the millions of his army covering the plains, and the thousands of his ships whitening the sea, and he thought how soon the living host would all moulder down to dust. Alexander of Macedon wept when he found himself the master of the world, and yet less satisfied than he was when he began the career of conquest. The hero of a hundred battles, the idolized commander of a half million of warriors, the autocrat of kings who cast down thrones and changed the destiny of nations, wept over the body of one poor soldier slain in his service.

There is something very awful in the tears as well as in the power and wrath of such mighty conquerors. They rule the destiny of millions. They make themselves the terror of nations. Their movements are watched, as men watch the progress of the pestilence in fear lest it shall come among them. By the flattery of friends and the fear of subjects they are exalted as gods. But their tears prove them to be men, weak, passionate, disappointed, helpless men.

But the tears of the Son of God wept at the grave of Lazarus, and over the impending woes of unhappy Jerusalem, have a far deeper and more awful meaning than the tears of human weakness, or humbled pride, or disappointed ambition. He did not weep because the mighty work which he had undertaken to do surpassed his power, or because the desire of his soul had failed to be satisfied. It is a most astonishing proof of the depth of his sympathy that he should weep with the afflicted while yet he possessed the power to restore the dead to life. He could bring back the lost treasure, but he could not be insensible to the grief of those who mourned as if it could never be recovered. However full and satisfying the consolation which he was able to bestow, he must weep with those who wept around him. So the mother subjects the little child to a brief disappointment, to inculcate the spirit of obedience, and yet she weeps from sympathy with the child's grief, while intending to bestow a richer gratification in the end. Jesus wept because the depth of his own sympathy made the grief which others felt as real to him as it was to them. This is the astonishing revelation which baffles all reason, and dazzles the vision of the loftiest faith; the sympathy of the infinite One with the grief of our poor hearts. There is nothing in prophecy, nothing in miracles, nothing in the whole creation, so new, so wonderful, so enrapturing as the expression of the divine pity in the tears of the weeping Son of God.

And then again, Jesus must have been moved by something more than the sorrow of the little company around him, when he groaned in spirit and was troubled even to tears. He saw indeed quite enough to make him weep in the affliction which death had brought upon one quiet and beloved family. But besides all that, he bore upon his heart the sorrows and the desolations of ages. His ear was open to the wail of the suffering and afflicted in all lands, in all times. To him, the woes of the whole human race broke forth in one exceeding great and bitter cry, and his soul was in agony to relieve them all. He could hear the moan of the great ocean of human grief breaking from its unsounded depths upon all the shores of time, and rolling the awful burden of sorrow into the abyss of eternity. He knew that the history of millions for ages to come, would be written in blood and blotted with tears.

He could comfort the bereaved sisters of Bethany by awakening their brother from the sleep of death. But the mighty miracle itself would be only a drop of consolation to the infinite ocean of human grief. The risen Lazarus must die again. The comforted sisters must mourn again. Themselves and all dear to them must die. The pitiless ravages of death must go on through all the earth. In the very hour when one was raised from the tomb, thousands would die. While the heart of Jesus was moved with infinite pity for all the afflicted and suffering, and with the desire to relieve them all, he knew how hard it would be to arrest the tide of human woe. While he was willing to give his own life-blood to put out the torturing fires of guilt and remorse in the human soul, he knew that even that sacrifice would fail to save many. All this sin and sorrow of a weeping and dying world, being represented to the mind of Jesus by the grief of the little company about him at Bethany, he wept. He groaned in spirit and was troubled.

The tears of Jesus, the deep and unaffected sorrow of the divine and holy Saviour, shows better than anything else how exceedingly evil and bitter a thing we have all done in forsaking the fountain of living waters. God might thunder denunciations against sin from the heavens every hour. He might write threatenings in letters of fire upon the sky every night. He might cause the earth to groan and belch forth fires in every land and the billows of the ocean to lift up their voices on every shore in wrathful testimony against transgression. And yet all that array of terror would not show us as deeply, as sadly as the tears of Jesus how dreadful a thing it is to sin, how hard a task it is for infinite power to save from the consequences of sin.

That a holy being should weep, that the Son of God should be troubled in spirit, that the divine Saviour should be bowed down with anguish and utter his sorrows in groans and tears, is indeed a mystery that may cause the heavens to wonder and the earth to be astonished. It can be explained only by admitting that the evil of sin is infinite, and that the salvation of sinners is a work for the utmost resources of infinite power. That mighty One who wept by the grave of Lazarus, could walk the waves, and hush the storm, and create abundance in the desert, and call to his aid legions of angels, and raise the dead. But he took on himself a greater task in becoming a Man of sorrows, and in bearing the sins of a lost world. In executing that great commission, he must destroy death. He must deliver those whom sin had bound in everlasting chains. He must spoil the powers of darkness and return to his heavenly throne, with redemption for the brightest of his many crowns. He must lift up the guilty and fallen from their degradation, make them equal with angels, sharers of his glory and kings forever unto God. And he must do all that in such a way as to maintain justice, and encourage obedience, to honor the divine law and to cover the pride and power of sin with everlasting contempt. No wonder that the Son of God himself, under the pressure of such a burden, groaned in spirit and wept with an anguish that was deeper than the utmost depths of human sorrow.

While then Jesus wept in sympathy with the little company of mourners around him, while his own heart felt the blow which had fallen upon his beloved friend, he wept still more bitterly for those who would not believe though the dead should come back to life before their eyes; for the deeper and more awful death by which the souls of millions were held in hopeless captivity to sin; for the madness of multitudes who should hear the word of life in their day of visitation and reject it; for the strange infatuation of those who should admit the truth of that word and pay all outward respect to its ministrations, and yet never receive it to their hearts; for the whole race of man, so slow to believe, so hard to be reclaimed, while countless woes in every land, and remorse in every heart testify to the need of a Saviour; for the one great apostacy from

God which has filled all human homes with sorrow, and loaded all the languages of men with words of woe, and enticed countless multitudes into the broad way of destruction, and peopled the regions of darkness with lost souls;—for this did Jesus weep; for this the heavens might well be dissolved in tears and the whole creation groan and travail in pain together. To arrest the progress of this world-wide and infinite woe, the Son of God wrestled in pain and sorrow till the sweat wrung out from his great agony fell like drops of blood upon the ground. For this he bowed himself at last in death upon the cross.

The words with which the evangelist describes the feelings of Jesus as he approached the tomb, express indignation, as well as grief. We ask at what the weeping and compassionate Saviour could be indignant at such a moment. We can only say that his anger burned against the cause which has done and will still do so much to fill the world with wailing and despair. He who could pour out his pity for sinners in flowing tears, must still regard sin itself as the fit subject of indignation and wrath. He was willing to suffer and die that the guilty might be saved, but he could not be indifferent to the enormity of their sin. And in the end, those who reject his offered love, will have nothing in the universe so much to fear as the displeasure of him who died for their salvation. They will pray to be covered by the rocks and mountains of a burning world rather than to meet the "wrath of the Lamb."

16. TAKE YE AWAY THE STONE.

And now Jesus, groaning in himself cometh to the grave. It was a cave and a stone lay upon it. The chief mourners gather closely around him, and curious spectators follow to hear what will be said and to see what will be done. This mighty Son of God whose voice the dead in their graves shall all hear, stands at the door of the tomb in which his beloved friend lies buried. But he pauses in the moment when all eyes are fixed upon him with the most intense and painful expectation, and he looks around him for human help. His infinite and divine power will not perform the mighty miracle of raising the dead, until human hands have performed the common and trifling task of taking away the stone.

He can summon legions of angels and they will come at his call. He can bid the mountains depart and the hills remove, and they will obey his word. But he stands at the tomb of his buried friend, as if his were the feeblest hand in all the company, and he says to those around him, "Take ye away the stone." His divine power will not display itself in the mighty work of raising the dead, unless the feeble, the afflicted, and the helpless shall perform their part and prepare the way. The stone lies heavy and cold at the door of the tomb, and the body of the buried Lazarus, lies as dead and cold within, yet the voice of the Son of God will not be heard by the silent sleeper; he will not know that Jesus stands so near, unless the helping hands of men shall roll away the stone.

The feeble faith of the afflicted fails them in the very moment when all their grief is about to be changed to a new and surprising joy. They interpose objections and hindrances in the way of Jesus, just as he is ready to speak the word which will lift the heaviest burden from their hearts. "Oh! no. Take not away the stone. We cannot bear to look upon the face of our brother, changed as it is now by the decay and the revolting ghastliness of death. We would remember him as we saw him in the pale and placid slumber of death, with the gentle smile, with which he bade us farewell, still lingering upon his lip. No, no, take not away the stone. It is too late. There is no trace of life or loveliness left upon the face of our beloved, and we cannot bear the sight."

So the broken-hearted mourners of Bethany hesitate and hold back the arm of infinite power, when Jesus stands before them and they have only to do his bidding and their lost brother shall be restored to life again. A word of his could cast that stone into the depths of the sea. But he pauses and reasons with the afflicted ones, and persuades them to permit him to help them in his own way and to use the aid which he chooses in his divine work. Infinite power and infinite mercy wait for the consent of human hearts and the help of human hands. If the afflicted will not take his word, if those who stand around will not put forth their effort as if divine power needed their aid, the miracle will not be performed, the dead will not be raised, the living will be left to mourn for their beloved as those who refuse to be comforted.

It is upon like conditions that Jesus still performs his mighty work of raising to spiritual life those who are dead in trespasses and in sins. There is much for human faith and human hands to do, before the cold dead world will hear the voice of the Son of God and wake to new life. Jesus comes and stands in the midst of communities and congregations, ready to speak the word which thousands must hear or never see life. But he turns to his friends, his followers, his consecrated and covenanted disciples, who have besought him to come, and he waits for them to take the cold and heavy stone of unbelief from their own hearts. He will awake the dead; he will make the nations hear his voice; he will fill the habitations of the living with the songs of ransomed and immortal millions, if only his followers will have faith in his presence and in his power to save.

There is many a city now as of old where Jesus is restrained from carrying on his mighty work of conversion and salvation, by the unbelief of his own disciples. If they could only have faith, they would see the glory of God in the coming forth of thousands to the new life of love and consecration to Christ. The sceptic may scoff, the indifferent may pass idly by, the curious may wonder and speculate, and none may dream that themselves are ever to be brought humbly and penitently to bow at the feet of Jesus. And yet they will hear his voice and he will make them all his own, as soon as his friends and followers venture to take him at his word when he says, "All things are possible to them that believe."

It is not money, nor talent, nor learning, nor opportunity so much as faith that the church needs to fulfil its great commission to make disciples of all nations. No arguments of the sceptic, no opposition of the wicked, no indifference of the worldly can stand before the truth speaking by the faith, and toil and sacrifice of a united and consecrated church. All the riches and power and glory of the earth shall be given to the followers of Christ, when once they have faith enough to give all they have to him. The world, that lies dead in trespasses and sins, shall hear the voice of the Son of God and come forth to new life, when the followers of Jesus arise at his command and roll away the stone of unbelief from their own hearts.

17. LIFE FROM THE DEAD.

And now the rock is rolled away, and the silent company stand before the open tomb, in the hush of breathless and awful expectation. The last act of human faith is done, and the believing mourners are waiting to see the glory of God. If the voice of Jesus avails in this case to call back the lost life, it must be a display of the same power which gives life to all creatures that live. The daughter of Jairus at Capernaum had been but a little while dead, when Jesus touched her hand, and her spirit came again. The grave had not yet received the young man, when Jesus touched the bier at the gate of Nain, and he that was dead rose up and began to speak. In such a case, the caviler might say that the apparent death was only a trance, and the asserted miracle of the restoration was only a natural waking from sleep.

But here is a grave opened so long after the burial, that living friends shrink from beholding the form of their beloved in decay. Here stands the Prince of life, face to face with the revolting aspect and the dread reality of death. Will he have power to make his voice heard, in that mysterious world where the soul of Lazarus has been so many days wandering or at rest? Will the dark kingdom of death throw open its inexorable doors, and permit its new subject to return, in answer to the call of the Son of man? Shall the emancipated spirit, having once escaped from its fetters and flown forth upon the boundless range of the universe, return at the command of Jesus, and consent to take up its old burden of suffering flesh, and tread the narrow round of its earthly prison-house again?

Such is the awful test to which the power,

the authority and the whole divine mission of Jesus are subjected, at the tomb of Lazarus. In the company of silent and wondering spectators that stand around, are represented the whole race of man held in bondage to death, and waiting to see whether the word of their offered Deliverer shall avail to throw open the doors of their prison-house, and set them free. If the departed soul of Lazarus comes not back at the call of Jesus, then there is no hope for man, and the wide world is given over to the endless and absolute dominion of death. If this changed and ghastly form, now as lifeless as the earth and rock of the tomb, shall respond to the voice of Jesus, and stand forth in the fullness of restored life, then surely all may live by faith in him. Trusting in this mighty Conqueror, we can triumph over the one great destroyer, whose presence has filled every earthly home with desolation, and whose dread has covered the unseen world with the pall of darkness and horror.

Imagining ourselves standing with the waiting company at the grave of Lazarus, and knowing that such mighty consequences depend upon the utterance of the word when Jesus cries with a loud voice, "COME FORTH," we are breathless with expectation. Like the weeping sisters, who most desired to see the face of their restored brother, we are almost afraid to have him speak the word which, when spoken, must confirm or extinguish our dearest hopes forever.

But Jesus himself is calm. He no longer weeps, now that he has the work of infinite power to do. His prayer unto his Father is a thanksgiving, and his call upon the dead is a command as quickly obeyed as spoken. The form, so changed with decay that friends feared to look upon it, stands forth before all the company a living man, waiting only to be loosed from his grave-clothes, to return to his home in the strength and beauty of his young manhood. It is not the slow recovery by which the dying sometimes come back, with feeble step and fainting breath, from the borders of the grave. It is not as when a strong man wakes suddenly from deep sleep, bewildered and lost. This deeper sleep of death passes instantaneously, at the word of Jesus, into full and conscious life. And again the mighty One, who has performed the divine work of restoration, looks around him for the help of human hands to loose the bands with which the dead was bound and let the living go.

So evermore must the human and divine co-operate in the mighty work of delivering captive souls from the bands of spiritual death. The voice of the Son of God alone can break the slumber of those who are dead in trespasses and sins. But human faith can do much to prepare the way for the divine work; and human effort must ever be put forth to improve and confirm the victory which divine power has gained.

Human curiosity searches the inspired record in vain, to find what recollections the restored Lazarus brought back from that unseen world where his spirit was wandering while his body rested in the tomb. It was not to gratify such curiosity that Jesus unbarred the gates of death and brought back the soul of his beloved friend. It was rather to prove beyond all question that the sceptre of his power is supreme over both worlds, and that those who trust in him can never go beyond the hearing of his voice or the reach of his hand.

The most acute of modern sceptics confesses that if the resurrection of Lazarus be a reality it demonstrates the divine authority of the whole Gospel, and shuts up every candid mind to the logical necessity of believing in Jesus as the Son of God and the Saviour of the world. It is only necessary that the sacred record shall be studied with the same faith and fairness which the severest critics accord to other portions of ancient history, in order that the reality of the resurrection may be established beyond question, and that this mighty miracle of Bethany may stand forth in complete and glorious demonstration of all that man need believe to be saved. This beloved and truthful man of Bethany, who came back from the unseen world at the word of Jesus, testifies by his life to all readers of the Gospel history, that Jesus is Lord both of the dead and the living. He has proved his power to destroy death, and with him for a friend the weak can conquer the mightiest foe, and the timid can face the king of terrors without fear.

Jesus raised the dead body of Lazarus to life, that all might trust in his power to restore spiritual life to those who are dead in trespasses and sins. He performs this greater miracle even now, before the eyes of men, whenever a weary, sin-burdened soul is drawn to him for rest. This new creation of fallen men to eternal life and glory by the power of Jesus is the great wonder which this material and doubting age finds it hardest to believe. The philosophy of the day undertakes the task of explaining all phenomena, both of the material and the spiritual world, without admitting the supernatural interference of divine power. Common life is taken up more and more with toil and hurry and social competition. And between the two extremes, there are too few to say, "We would see Jesus." There is too little sensibility to the awful and glorious truth that divine power is still in the world to make a new creation of spiritual life in the hearts of men, as instantaneously as Lazarus came forth from the tomb at the word of Jesus. And yet all the true progress of the world towards a higher and better life, must spring from a more full acceptance of this divine theory of spiritual creation, according to which the dead in trespasses and sins are made new creatures in Christ Jesus. The power to make wicked men holy, to change the ruling purpose of the heart from bad to good, is more needed for the improvement of mankind, than the power to multiply the productions of the earth, the inventions of art, or the discoveries of science. When once Christ has brought men into sympathy with himself by the mighty appeal of his cross, they become joint-heirs with him of the whole boundless creation, and they have before them the ages of eternity in which to enjoy their possessions.

When Jesus performed the great miracle of Bethany, he took a decisive step towards the appointed completion of his earthly life. The work was seen by jealous eyes, and it was soon reported in all Jerusalem, with such comments as malice and falsehood could make. His enemies saw that what they did for his destruction, must be done quickly; for they could not long inflame the passions of the people against one, who could call the dead from the grave in the open light of day, in the presence of many witnesses, and with the power of a single word. From that day forth they took counsel together how they might put him to death. But his hour was not yet fully come. He must make one circuit more of instruction and mercy, upon the borders of Samaria and Galilee, and when he returns, two months later, to Bethany for the last time, the great week of his passion has already begun. From this mountain village, where he restored the dead to life, he must go forth to his own death. From this quiet home where he had been received so many times with loving hospitality, he must pass through the mockeries of Jerusalem and the agony of the cross, to his Father's house and his heavenly throne.

JERUSALEM.

Behold, we go up to Jerusalem; and the Son of man shall be betrayed unto the chief priests and unto the scribes, and they shall condemn him to death, and shall deliver him to the Gentiles to mock, and to scourge and to crucify him.—MATT. xx. 18, 19.

VIII.
JERUSALEM.

DRIVEN from Bethlehem by the wrath of a king, expelled from Nazareth by the violence of the people, received at Capernaum at first only to be rejected at last, denied the protection of the three homes which were his by birth, by residence, and by adoption, Jesus comes to Jerusalem to be betrayed and to Calvary to die. Thirty years of retirement, and three years of public ministry are all that the world will endure of its Messiah. It is not enough to secure him acceptance that he heals the sick, and feeds the hungry, and raises the dead. It is not enough that he speaks as never man spake, and does the works which no man ever did, and endures the contradiction of sinners with the meekness and majesty of infinite love.

He must go down to a still lower depth in

humiliation; he must take upon his soul the burden of a greater agony; he must give his very life in sacrifice, before the stony walls of prejudice and hatred and unbelief will yield and give him access to the hearts of men. The testimony of the divine love must be confirmed by the infinite argument of the cross, before the world will accept its own Redeemer or consent to be saved.

We cannot observe our Lord too closely while he is passing through the closing scenes of his earthly life. We have something to learn from every step which he takes, in his firm and sure approach to the great sacrifice of Calvary.

1. THE TRIUMPHAL ENTRY.

His first entrance into Jerusalem on the solemn week of his passion, has the appearance of a triumph. He had walked up the wild and weary road from Jericho and from the Fords of the Jordan to Bethany, and had spent his last earthly Sabbath at the house of his friends in that mountain village. It was the week of the Passover, and multitudes of pilgrims were on their way from Galilee, to keep the great festival in the Holy city. Some remained with him at Bethany on the day of rest; many passed over the brow of Olivet and encamped in the gardens and orchards on the western slope of the mountain, every where spreading the tidings that the Prophet of Nazareth was two miles off at Bethany, and would appear in the city before the feast had closed.

On the afternoon of Sunday, the first day of the Jewish week, Jesus renewed his journey, accompanied by a great multitude from Bethany, who were eager to witness his reception in the city. He set forth knowingly and willingly to meet his death, when the new life of the year had come, and the whole land was green and blossoming with the glory of spring. Taking the most traveled road over the southern ridge of Olivet, he was joined by a still greater multitude, who had heard of his coming, and had gone forth from the camps on the hill-sides and from the streets of Jerusalem to meet him. When the two great processions met, the one which came from the direction of the city turned and went before, and the other which started out from Bethany followed, with Jesus in the midst, and, both united, rent the air with shouts that were heard in all the streets

and on all the hill-sides round about Jerusalem. Branches were broken from the palms by the way-side and hastily braided into mattings to carpet the road. Others still more enthusiastic threw off their outer garments and spread them in the way to be trodden upon by the beast that bore the Son of David. And so far were the excited multitude from exaggerating the greatness of the occasion by their shouts and demonstrations of joy, that Jesus himself said, the stones would immediately cry out were the people to hold their peace.

Rounding the southern ridge of the mountain, and coming out upon a level platform of rock, Jesus beheld, across the deep ravine of the Kidron, the whole magnificent city in one full and instantaneous view. Conspicuous above everything else the golden domes and pinnacles of the temple rise before him like the flame of a mighty sacrifice. The whole mass of compact streets and stone houses within the walls, is crowded with people, and among the gardens and vineyards on all the hill-sides facing the city are encamped thousands upon thousands who have come up to the great national Feast. All this vast population is moved at his coming, and the multitude around him lift up their voices in cries of welcome, so loud that some within the city walls, hearing the sound said, "The world has gone after him."

At this moment of supreme triumph, Jesus weeps. Not for himself, although he well knew that before that week should close, the hosannas of the multitudes would give place to the cry, "crucify him." Not because his work had failed and his mission must close in defeat and disappointment. He weeps over doomed and blinded Jerusalem, because she knows not the time of her visitation. He weeps because the last and utmost appeal which he can make to the hearts of men by his death on the cross will still be rejected by many to their own destruction. He weeps because many, by continued impenitence and unbelief, would bring on themselves wrath unto the uttermost, when they might have been saved with a full and everlasting salvation.

And so Jesus begins the great week of his passion with triumph and with tears. The earthly triumph will soon be past. But it will give place to another, when he shall have led captivity captive, and the angelic host shall form the dazzling procession, and the everlasting gates of heaven shall be lifted up that the king of glory may come in. The sorrow with which Jesus weeps over Jerusalem, shall give place to joy, when he shall look back upon the travail of his soul, and be satisfied with the fruits of his toil and suffering.

2. STEPS TOWARDS THE CROSS.

From this time forward, Jesus pursued the open and avowed course which he knew must

bring him to the cross. For a time he had avoided publicity, and had kept himself out of the reach of those who were plotting together at Jerusalem, to put him to death. But now the work of teaching is done, the evidences of his divine mission are complete, and he goes voluntarily to put himself in the way of his enemies, that their malice may become the instrument of completing the great sacrifice for the world's redemption.

Descending the western slope of Olivet and crossing the Kidron, Jesus entered the city at St. Stephen's gate, and went up and showed himself in the courts of the temple, with the singing and shouting multitudes still around him. The whole city was moved. The scribes read the law with none to listen, and the priests were left alone with the evening sacrifice, for everybody had joined the eager crowd that were swaying and surging to and fro in the endeavor to see and to hear the Prophet of Nazareth.

Having looked around silently upon all things, Jesus left the temple and the city, and returned to Bethany for the night. The first decisive step towards the great sacrifice had been taken. He had shown himself the object of supreme interest to the multitude, and so had excited the envy and hatred of their customary leaders to the highest degree. He had come once more within their reach, and they were already intent upon new plans to destroy him. It will take them yet four days more to complete their dark counsels, and then when they demand the victim, he will hold himself ready for the sacrifice.

Monday he came back to the city, and made a still more striking exhibition of the power of his presence over men, by causing all that bought and sold in the temple to leave the holy place, and to take their tables and merchandise with them at his command. Hardened, selfish and calculating as they were, they could not withstand the authority with which he spoke. The blind, the sick and the lame were brought to him in great numbers and he healed them. The populace had been induced by threats or persuasion to hold their peace, but the children in the temple took up the songs and the cries of the previous day, and sung, "Hosanna to the Son of David." When the priests and the scribes demanded his authority for what he did, he put them to shame before all the people by the wisdom of his reply. And so when evening was come, he went back to Bethany, leaving them still more enraged and intent upon seeking his death.

3. THE LAST DAY OF PUBLIC TEACHING.

Tuesday, he came again to the city and this was his last day of public teaching. His enemies assailed him in greater numbers and with greater subtility than ever before. When one was silenced another would renew the assault, all alike endeavoring to ensnare him in his words, and to draw from him some expression which could be used as an accusation against him before the magistrates. But all in vain. They only induced him to set forth before all the people, by new parables and in a more awful light, the dreadful doom which they would bring on themselves, on the temple and the holy city, by rejecting their own Messiah. He pronounced the most fearful woes upon the blind and bigoted leaders of the people in their hearing and then left them. This was enough. The priests and scribes will see to it that the dreaded voice of their Reprover shall not be heard in the courts of the temple, or in the streets of the city any more. To-night the great council will meet in secret session at the palace of the high priest, and the betrayer will be there, to bargain for the reward of iniquity, in delivering Jesus into their hands.

4. THE LAST LOOK AT JERUSALEM.

On his way out to Bethany that evening, Jesus paused before passing the ridge of Olivet and sat down with his disciples, over against the temple, to look back upon Jerusalem for the last time. The sun was setting, and the whole city, with the surrounding valleys and hill-sides alive with the camps of pilgrims, lay beneath him in the evening light. The history of a thousand years, the divine oracles speaking by a thousand voices, the monuments of prophets, patriarchs and kings, the visitations of angels, miraculous interpositions in judgment and in blessing, from the offering of Isaac and the building of the temple, were present to him, as he looked upon Moriah and Zion, and heard the murmur and the evening songs of a million people gathered within and around the walls of the holy city. Nowhere on earth was it possible to find another scene of such commanding interest as that which lay before the eye of Jesus, when he turned to look upon Jerusalem for the last time. And there he sat till the sun went down and the stars shone, and the already risen moon grew bright over the mountains of Moab. There he poured forth, in the most solemn and touching words, prophecy and warning and instruction, concerning the desolation of Jerusalem, the dispersion of the Jewish people, the preaching of the gospel to all nations, and his own final coming to judge the world in righteousness. He closed this, the most awful and sublime of all his discourses, with the distinct and solemn declaration that after two days he should be betrayed and crucified. Then he resumed his walk to Bethany and rested for the night.

5. THE REPOSE OF PREPARATION.

The whole of the following day, Wednesday, he spent in retirement at his chosen and quiet home in Bethany. His public work was done, and while his enemies were completing their plans for his destruction, he would take a little time to gird up his soul for the trial of mockery and scourging, and for the crowning agony of the cross. He would need the repose of two quiet days to prepare himself for the last sleepless night, and for the long torture of the last dreadful day. When he leaves the quiet village for the last time on Thursday afternoon, he goes to be betrayed and crucified. His whole body and soul and spirit will be tasked with the most exhausting and unceasing intensity, until he bows his head in death at the ninth hour, on Friday afternoon.

6. THE LAST NIGHT.

As the evening of Thursday draws near, Jesus sets forth upon his last walk with his disciples before his passion. We do not know what words of farewell were spoken when he parted with his beloved friends at Bethany, they fondly hoping to see him return to lodge with them as before, and he well knowing that his next resting place would be the grave. We are not told what he said to his disciples as he walked with them up the same steep, or down the same descent of Olivet, where the multitudes hailed his coming with hosannas four days before. We do not know whether in silence, or with weeping, or with comforting words, he passed Gethsemane and crossed the Kidron, and climbed up the ascent to St. Stephen's gate. But from the moment of his arrival at the upper chamber in the city, where the passover was prepared, we may well imagine that his countenance wore an unwonted tenderness and solemnity, and that the wondering disciples saw the foreshadowing signs of the final agony upon him. The awful history of this last night and the following day, will be studied with wonder and adoration by angels and by redeemed men forever. We can now only recite its most familiar facts as a preparation for the lessons of the cross, with which this book must close.

Just about to complete his earthly humiliation and to return to the throne of heaven with all power in his hands and all glory upon his head, Jesus teaches his disciples the greatness of humility. While they are contending

with each other for the highest place in his promised kingdom, he girds himself as a servant and washes the feet of them that call him Lord. Just about to offer himself, the pure and spotless Lamb of God, in the great and only efficacious sacrifice for sin, he finishes the sacrifices of four thousand years by eating the Passover with his disciples. In place of the national festival which the Jewish people had observed from the days of Moses, he institutes a memorial service, to be kept by his followers of every nation to the end of time. As he looks around upon the chosen company of his disciples, the dark shadow of coming treachery overclouds and troubles his soul, and groaning within himself, he nerves his heart to make the sad declaration, "Verily, verily, I say unto you, that one of you shall betray me." The disclosure makes the company of the disciples and the presence of the Master intolerable to the traitor. He goes immediately out, and it is night—night in the streets of blinded and abandoned Jerusalem, night in the councils of the enemies of Jesus, night in the soul of the betrayer, night upon the path which he must tread forever.

No sooner has the dark shadow of the traitor's presence left the room, than the troubled cloud passes from the face of Jesus and he turns to his remaining disciples with the light of heaven in his look. And now he pours forth his soul in words of love, of counsel and of prayer which shall outlive the languages of earth, and shall be sung by blest voices to the music of heaven. He himself joins with his disciples in singing the great Hallelujah song with which Israel had closed the Passover for a thousand years, "Praise the Lord all ye nations, praise him all ye people, for his merciful kindness is great towards us, his mercy endureth forever."

He knows where the betrayer will expect to find him at the midnight hour, and thither he goes that he may be ready when the officers and soldiers come with Judas for their guide to take him. Once more through the silent street and out of the Eastern gate, and across the Kidron valley, beneath the shadows which olive trees cast in the full moonlight, Jesus

goes to his place of prayer. The betrayer knew the spot, for Jesus had often been there before with his disciples. To this day, in spite of all intervening changes, the scene can be identified with reasonable accuracy, and it is the most solemn and affecting of all the "holy places" in Palestine. The aged olive trees, with gnarled and distorted trunks, appearing as if bent and twisted with the torture of centuries are the most fitting monument, if anything be needed to mark the sacred ground.

While waiting for the armed band to appear, Jesus is again troubled in spirit, and his soul is bowed down under the weight of a more awful and mysterious agony than had ever come upon him before. He is overcome with a strange amazement, an inexplicable and shuddering dread, a horror of great darkness, an exceeding great sorrow embittered with more than the bitterness of death. The sweat, wrung out from the inward torture, falls in bloody drops upon the ground. Thrice he prays in the same words that the cup may pass from him. And it seems a relief from something worse when the armed band appears, and he goes forth to give himself up. His troubled countenance at once assumes so much of its serene and godlike majesty, that the hardened soldiers are struck to the ground with awe before him. But the delay is only momentary. He offers himself again, and they bind him and lead him away.

It is now past midnight, and from this time forward the course of events in this awful history runs swiftly on to the closing scene on the cross. First walking painfully with bound hands amid the rude and merciless mob, Jesus is hurried down and up the steep path, through the city gate to the house of Annas. Not for a formal trial did they bring him there, but only that the old father-in-law of the high priest, the man whose counsel was of the highest authority in the nation, might have the dreadful satisfaction of seeing Jesus of Nazareth a prisoner. Then out again into the dark, narrow streets, finding their way by the uncertain light of lanterns and torches, they hurry their unresisting victim with insults and mockery to the palace of Caiaphas.

Here he is questioned by the high priest, testified against by false witnesses, smitten by the officers, reviled by the whole assembly, condemned to death by the council, and still after the decision, kept exposed to every form of contemptuous speech and personal abuse, till the break of day. And while he is subjected to such mockery from his enemies, the heart of Jesus is pierced with a deeper pang, by hearing his own honored and foremost disciple Peter deny, with bitter oaths and blasphemy, that he ever knew him.

The morning of Friday breaks, a day to be recorded as the greatest of all the days of time; a day to be remembered long as redeemed souls remember the sacrifice which purchased for them a blessed immortality. The sentence of the Sanhedrim must now be confirmed, and executed by the civil power, or it will be of no effect. And the enemies of Jesus hurry on their dreadful work with such malignant and impetuous zeal, that their prisoner, who was seized in Gethsemane, without the city, at midnight, has been led to and fro through many streets, to four different palaces or tribunals, has been arraigned twice before the high priests, twice before the Sanhedrim, twice before Pilate, once before Herod, has been once robed and crowned in mockery, twice scourged, everywhere mocked and condemned, led out of the city wall, and by nine o'clock, when the sun is looking over the ridge of Olivet into the deep valley of the Kidron, he is already nailed to the cross. In six hours more, the most momentous hours in the world's history, the awful tragedy is finished, and the incarnate Son of God bows his head in death.

It is all one act, one mysterious and infinite passion, from the agony in Gethsemane to the last bitter cry upon Calvary. The betrayal, the arrest, the arraignment, the false accusation, the mockery, the denial, the scourging, the final sentence and its execution, must all unite to make up the meaning of that most sacred and awful mystery, the cross of Christ.

The most sorrowful procession that ever moved on this earth, was that in which Jesus was led out of the city to be crucified, amid the wail of the daughters of Jerusalem, and the mockery of the multitude that clamored for his death. But we cannot describe the street along which the procession passed. We do not know where the cross was set up. And it is well that we do not, else the spot might draw even spiritual worshippers to itself, rather than to him by whose sufferings it was consecrated.

What we do know of the death of Christ, is of far greater importance to us than the precise spot or time of his crucifixion. If the material cross itself were miraculously multiplied and set up as an object of reverence in every Christian sanctuary, it might only degrade our conceptions of the spiritual cross, and divert our trust from the living, immortal Christ himself, to things that change and pass away.

Nevertheless it will do us all good, frequently and solemnly to review the closing scenes in the Saviour's earthly life. Amid all the material and worldly passions, by which we are beset and tempted, we shall learn many salutary lessons, by going back in memory, and spending a thoughtful hour, in the endeavor to strengthen our faith and quicken our love at the foot of the cross. What then are the lessons which the divine Passion, the infinite sacrifice, the true and redemptive Cross of Christ is fitted to teach?

7. THE LESSONS OF THE CROSS.

First of all we may learn that lesson which is the beginning of life and peace to weary souls, the lesson of penitence at the foot of the cross. It was for our sins that Christ was lifted up. It was to save us from shame and everlasting contempt, that he consented to have the scorn and mockery of the world heaped upon him. It was the thick cloud of our transgressions, that poured darkness upon his soul, and extorted from him the cry, as of one smitten and forsaken of God. He was put to grief and he carried our sorrows, that he might pour the oil of gladness into our stricken hearts, and that God's own hand might wipe away all tears from our eyes forever. He consented to be numbered among transgressors, and to make his soul an offering for sin, that we might be justified before God, that all our wanderings might be healed, and that we might be restored to our Father's house and find rest and peace forever.

And if anything will move our hearts to penitence for our sins, it must be the great sight of the incarnate Son of God, seen by faith, lifted up on the cross, and suffering that we might be saved, treated as a transgressor that we might be forgiven, dying that we might live and be alive for evermore. Everything that is generous, noble and manly in our nature must move us to sorrow for our sins, when we see how much an infinitely generous and holy Saviour is willing to suffer for our sake.

Sometimes it is enough to break the hard heart of a wicked son when he sees an affectionate and faithful mother mourning over his misconduct, smitten with grief for the shame and ruin which he is bringing on himself. He knows that it is only from generous and self-sacrificing love for him that his mother's heart bleeds. And it makes him seem to himself worse than a brute to be insensible while she is so deeply moved in his behalf. The only tie that has saved many a son from profligacy and destruction, has been the bond of love which bound him to a mother's heart.

But the love of Jesus is infinitely more generous, patient and self-denying than a mother's love. He has been more deeply afflicted by our ingratitude and disobedience than any mother ever was by the misconduct of her child. He has longed and labored for our eternal salvation more earnestly than any human parent ever did for the welfare of an only son.

As we stand and gaze by faith upon the cross of Jesus, every expression of his agonized countenance, every drop of blood flowing from his many wounds, every convulsion with which the torture of crucifixion shakes his frame, every groan which the hiding of his Father's face extorts from his troubled soul, seems to say to us, "It is for thee that these pangs are borne. It is that thou mayest be forgiven that I consent to have all shames and crimes imputed to me. It is to blot out the record of thy dark and dreadful iniquity that my blood is shed. The grave shall close over me with its horror of great darkness that I may spoil the dominions of death and unbar the gates of life for thee. I submit to all this shame and agony because I have loved thee with an everlasting love, and I could not rest till I had brought back thy wayward and wandering soul to God."

With such tender entreaty does the cross of Christ plead with every one of us against our sins, the moment we actually believe that he died for us. This one appeal has produced in the rude savage and the cultivated sceptic, the gentleness of the lamb and the docility of the child. And who would not mourn and be in bitterness of soul for his sins, when he sees them laid upon the holy Son of God and the meek and mighty sufferer is crushed to the very grave by the load? When reason fails to convince, when warning and invitation have been heard in vain, when chastisement and blessing have been equally slighted, when the hope of heaven no longer allures and the fear of punishment has lost its power, then still may the infinite generosity of Jesus in suffering for sinners touch the heart and unseal the fountain of tears.

And when we desire deeper conviction, when we wish to be more penitent, and wonder that we have so little sorrow for our sins, then we must come nearer to the cross. We must consider more earnestly the shame and the glory, the life and the death, the justice and the mercy that so meet and harmonize in the cross, that God is just and the guilty are forgiven, Jesus dies and sinners live, shame is poured upon the Son of the Highest and the ransomed soul is crowned with eternal glory. Thus, studying anew the great mystery of innocence suffering for the guilty, weighing again the mighty argument by which divine Love convinces of sin, we shall the more fervently offer the sacrifice of a broken and a contrite heart, which God will not despise. And he who will not take his fitting place, in humble penitence at the foot of the cross, may possess all that the world can give and yet be poor, he may learn all that the world can teach, and yet never become wise unto salvation.

We may learn the lesson of humility, as we go back by faith and stand on the mount of the great expiation. Who is this helpless victim nailed in agony to the accursed tree? Nay, call him not helpless. He could summon legions of God's mighty angels to his assistance with a word. He could doom all his enemies to everlasting destruction in a moment. He could make all the powers and terrors of the universe swift ministers to execute his vengeance, while his wrath was kindled but a little.

And yet he gives himself, as a lamb to the slaughter. When reviled he threatens not. When accused by false witnesses, he opens not his mouth. On the cross itself, he prays for those that nailed him there. Cruel Roman and scoffing Jew unite to torture his life, and to dishonor his death, and yet he gives himself to be smitten and scorned without a murmuring word. And this unresisting, uncomplaining victim is the Son of God. This is he whose throne is from everlasting, and whose kingdom shall have no end. The darkened heavens, the quaking earth, and the rising dead attest the divinity which man denies.

Come then, ye proud and vainglorious, whose hearts are ever panting for some petty distinction above your fellow-men, estimate the value of the highest earthly glory, while seeing the Son of God rejected and despised for your sake. Come, ye rich, and take account of all your perishable possessions within sight of that blood which was shed as a ransom for your sins. Come, ye complainers and murmurers, who are ever at conflict with the ways of providence and the will of your fellow-men; repeat the tale of your wrongs and sufferings, within hearing of the voice which prays for revilers and murderers,—"Father, forgive them, for they know not what they do." Come, ye passionate and contentious, whose anger kindles with provocation as the flax kindles in the flame; see, with what unmurmuring meekness, the Son of God endures the contradiction of sinners, and learn from him to pour contempt on all your pride. Come, ye poor and needy, who are tempted to envy the rich and to think that every earthly blessing can be bought with money; see to what a depth of destitution Christ submits for your sake, and learn from the cross to prize above all earthly possessions, the inheritance of life which he impoverished himself to purchase and to bestow on you.

And if any of us are ever to subdue the pride and vanity of our hearts, if we are ever to bring ourselves into familiar and holy converse with things unseen and eternal, we must learn to estimate all human interests in the light which shines from the cross. We must fathom the depths of the humiliation to which the Son of God submitted, that he might raise us up from our fallen state. We must consider how great the sacrifice which he must needs make in his own person, to bring back our wandering souls to his Father's house. We must lay open our hearts to the mighty constraint of that love, which could come forth from the throne of heaven, and search through all the wastes of sin and misery to recover the lost. While thus looking with penitence and trust upon him whom our sins have pierced and our sorrows have touched, we shall acquire strength to overcome the world. Standing fast in the great liberty wherewith the cross has set us free, we shall rejoice to bring every thought and desire into willing and happy captivity to the obedience of Christ.

The cross of Christ displays the character of God in the most attractive light. If it were not for the cross, we should not know our Father in heaven. We should not dare to call ourselves children of the Most High. We should not dare to ascribe to the supreme and eternal Judge, the relentings and compassions of an earthly parent's heart. Our present life would be a pitiless and hopeless orphanage, and the hour of death would be the beginning of endless despair.

But when we see the glory of the eternal Father shining in the face of the divine and co-eternal Son, we are attracted by infinite grace and benignity, we rejoice in the accents of paternal love. Without the cross of Christ, we never could believe that the infinite One pities our infirmities as a human father pities his own children. We might concede, as a logical necessity, the existence of one supreme Creator and Governor of the universe. We might discern many evidences of his wisdom and power in the world around us. But we should not know that we had a Father to love us, with infinite and everlasting love, to pity us with a parent's tender pity, to draw us to himself with more than a mother's yearning toward a wayward child.

It is only when we come near to the cross of Jesus, that we see the infinite God manifesting such paternal tenderness and condescension towards us. Every pang, every degree of shame that the holy and the divine Redeemer suffers for our sake, teaches us better than a thousand arguments, that God is love, that he loves *us*, and that he has given his Son for our salvation, with a father's affectionate and self-forgetting generosity. This is the great revelation of the cross, the holy and the mighty God, the Maker of all worlds and the absolute Arbiter of all destinies, revealed as a compassionate and forgiving Father.

And this knowledge of God is worth infinitely more to us, than all that the schools of philosophy can teach about the Creator and Governor of the universe. We see only one side of the character of God, when we contemplate his greatness and power, his justice and truth.

His greatness might not condescend to our feebleness, and then we should be desolate and helpless. His power might crush us, as we tread by accident or by design upon a worm in the dust, and then we are ruined. His justice is terrible to us, because we are sinners. His truth exposes our guilt and puts us to shame forever.

But when we look to the crucified One of Calvary for all that we need most to know of God, when we study the divine character in the light of the cross, we see mercy, tenderness and forgiveness blending harmoniously with the awful attributes of holiness, justice and power, and then we find a Father in him of whom our sins made us afraid. Instead of fleeing from him, we rush to his arms for protection. The throne that was high and terrible to us in our unbelief, becomes beautiful and wondrously attractive, when we behold in the midst of it, One bearing the signs of having suffered for us, and we hide ourselves beneath its shadow when the storm of vengeance threatens to sweep us away.

O most glorious revelation of God which

shows us a Father, infinite and most holy, yet forgiving and reconciling us to himself by the cross. O, most excellent knowledge of Jesus Christ which reveals the hidden depths of sin in our hearts, and yet shows us the writing of the finger of God on the cloud of vengeance, "Live, O ye guilty and penitent souls, live for I have found a ransom." The deep and angry darkness which overhung our future pathway is transfigured and changed to glory in the light of revealed mercy. We see the shining domes and the sapphire walls of the heavenly city outlined upon the horizon where the sun of this earthly life goes down. The infinite gulf of perdition, which sin had disclosed yawning across our pathway, is bridged over by the cross, and redeemed souls pass in safety with songs and everlasting joy. We join the glorious company, and thenceforth the journey of life is only a return to our Father's house. Everything great and awful in the character of God puts on an aspect of beauty and attraction, and we are supremely drawn to him of whom in our sinful and unbelieving state we were most afraid.

To see God in such a character, we must gather around the cross. Christ and him crucified must become the great and commanding theme of our most earnest thought and of our most joyful emotion. Salvation by the blood of the Lamb must be fully accepted as the great inheritance of the future and the infinite compensation for all the losses and afflictions of this present time. The sorest chastisements become precious and blessed to us the moment we see from whom they come, and for what purpose they are sent. Believing that Christ was crucified for our sins, we ask no greater pledge of our Father's love; we cannot be told more plainly that the burden of our sins and sorrows has been laid upon One who is merciful to forgive and mighty to save. We can receive everything with gratitude from that hand which was nailed to the cross, we can trust everything to that love which could die that we might live.

This great mystery of the cross explains all other mysteries, and is itself dark to our vision only from excess of light. The doubting dare not receive it because it means so much. The philosopher will not receive it because it puts all his proud theories to shame. The worldling will not receive it because it draws and persuades and commands with such awful authority to a spiritual and a holy life. But all who look to Christ for the fullest revelation of the divine glory, find that it is the blessedness of life to believe in him; blessed to follow wherever Christ leads the way; blessed to bear whatever burdens Christ imposes; blessed to die in the hope of a resurrection which shall reveal Christ as he is upon the throne of heaven, coequal with the Father, and clothed with the glory that he had before the world was.

If, then, we would see the character of God in its most complete and gracious manifestation; if we would find out the meaning of that great and precious name, OUR FATHER; if we would know the exceeding greatness of the inheritance which that Father freely bestows upon his redeemed and adopted children we must look in faith upon the cross and so begin the study which shall be "the science and the song of all eternity." We must believe that Christ crucified is our living, personal and divine Saviour; that all he suffered was for our sake; that his sacrificial death is the great revelation which God makes of himself to the understanding and the heart; and then we shall have a higher wisdom than the great masters in human philosophy ever taught. We shall have acquired possessions more precious than all the riches of the earth can buy, a pure heart, a peaceful conscience and a hope that can conquer death.

We must look to the cross to learn the worth of the human soul, the true value and greatness of man. The question of our own immortality and of our capacity for endless blessedness beyond the grave, is settled at once and forever, the moment we see Jesus as he is. Beholding the incarnate Son of the Highest nailed in agony to the accursed tree, we see in a clearer light than any reasoning can show, the punishment due to transgression of the divine law, the infinite evil of sin in itself, the utter and endless ruin that awaits the wanderer from God.

For whom does this divine Saviour suffer

and die? For what purpose does he give himself to such terrible shame and agony? Is it for a child of the dust whose life begins and ends with earth and time? Is it for the rescue of souls from dangers that imagination creates? Is it for the forgiveness of sins that can never deserve the doom of eternal death?

Oh! no. This infinite and awful sacrifice of Calvary could be offered only for the redemption of a soul that was infinitely precious. This great ransom could be paid only for deliverance from endless and immitigable despair. The great creating Father, infinitely rich as he is in all the resources of wisdom and power, would not give his only begotten Son to death, unless the sacrifice were attended with a compensation that would fill the universe with praise and endure throughout all ages. The Redeemer himself could not be satisfied with the travail of his soul in suffering for sinners, unless the fruits of his conflict with the powers of darkness should be glory and joy forever and ever.

And such is the greatness of man, such is the value of one human soul, that the almighty

Father is satisfied with the infinite price which he pays for our salvation in the death of his own Son. It was for the joy set before him in accomplishing so great a salvation that Christ himself endured the cross, despising the shame. So awful was the doom from which sinners needed to be saved, so exalted and lasting the glory which they might attain if redeemed, that God was pleased to lay our iniquities upon his holy and beloved Son, and to put him to grief for our sake. And we may be sure that infinite love itself would not have submitted to such a sacrifice, had it not been to save us from the greatest conceivable woe; had it not been to display wisdom and mercy in such fulness as to fill the universe of holy beings with gratitude and praise.

And our own greatness, the infinite price at which God estimates the value of the human soul, is best seen in the greatness of the ransom paid for our redemption. If we possessed the treasures and revenues of empire, if we could command the riches and glories of the whole earth it would be infinite loss to give them all in exchange for the inheritance of life which is freely offered to us all through the blood of the cross. There was but one being in the universe great and mighty enough to bestow a title to that high estate upon the worthless and the guilty, and he could do it only by making his own soul an offering for sin.

We often hear it asked how much is a man worth? To answer that question we must go to Calvary. In the mystery and glory of the cross, we can best learn the price at which God estimates the value of man, any man, the poorest and lowliest on earth; for it was for such that the great sacrifice of the cross was made. How much is a man worth? I will tell you when you estimate for me the height of that glory from which Christ came down to die that man might be saved. I will tell you when you have told me how many worlds are upheld by the power of him who cried in agony upon the cross, "My God, my God, why hast thou forsaken me?" I will tell you when you have counted for me the everlasting years during which Christ had reigned above all thrones and powers, when he bowed his head in death, saying, "It is finished."

I will tell how much the poorest and most unfriended man in all the world is worth, when you have measured for me the height and depth and length and breadth of the love of Christ, displayed in man's redemption; when you have searched through all the deeps of the prison-house of despair, and summed up all the wailings of lost souls in the habitation of darkness; when you have heard every voice, and measured the joy of every heart that shall sing the song of redemption forever and ever; when you have estimated the flood of glory and gladness, that shall be poured upon the universe of immortal beings, by the redeeming work of Christ in the endless ages to come; when you have felt and comprehended the infinite joy with which the Redeemer himself rejoices over the salvation of the lost; when you have done all this I will tell you how much the poorest man on earth is worth.

And I should need to have all these estimates made for me, and I should need the faculty to comprehend the infinite result, before I could tell how many and how strong are the reasons, why any one individual man should trust in Christ for the salvation of his own soul. No process of reasoning, no impassioned appeal, no cry of alarm can set forth the danger of delay in repentance, the immensity of the hazard in rejecting the offered salvation but once, in so awful a light as it is seen by one earnest look at the cross, one distinct and full recognition of the incarnate Son of God, in the crucified one of Calvary.

The cross was originally the symbol of the utmost shame, and crucifixion was the reality of the utmost torture that the world could inflict. Christ endured both the shame and the agony, because he knew the riches of the glory of the inheritance lost by sin; he knew the greatness of the ransom that must be paid for the recovery of the forfeited possession. And there is nothing on earth more sorrowful than to see men anxious to secure trifling and perishable possessions, yet indifferent to the loss of eternal life; grateful for a momentary attention from a human friend, yet insensible to the infinite generosity of the Son of God in dying for their salvation.

The cross teaches the great lesson of trust

and consecration. As I go back in imagination to the scene of the great sacrifice, and mingle in the company that stand to gaze, methinks I hear the voice of some one spectator, more serious and attentive than the rest, saying—" Is this in very deed the Son of God? And is it for my sins that he suffers and dies this awful death? And does he endure all this just because he desires to save me from all guilt and shame and suffering, and to make me blessed forever? Then the homage of my heart and the service of my hands shall be his forever. All that I have is too little to give to one who so loved me as to give himself, his whole, divine, eternal self for me. I cannot trust such a Saviour too much, I cannot give myself to his service with too deep a devotion.

> "Were the whole realm of nature mine,
> That were a present far too small:
> Love so amazing, so divine,
> Demands my soul, my life, my all."

And a believing view of the cross may well awaken such sentiments of trust and consecration in every heart. Christ gives himself our ransom from sin and death. Shall we think our poor unworthy selves too much to give for him? He suffers for us, shall we refuse to be made happy in his service? He dies for us, is it too much for us to live for him? He consents to be crucified in shame that we may be crowned with eternal glory. He becomes a servant that we may be made kings unto God and reign forever. And shall men choose everlasting bondage to sin and death, rather than be bound to Christ in bonds of love, and live with him in the glorious liberty of a redeemed and blessed immortality?

The cross supplies us with our one unfailing source of hope, glory and joy. Taking the crucifixion as the evidence and measure of God's sympathy with us, there is no depth of affliction, no hour of darkness and temptation in which we cannot glory and rejoice. This most surpassing revelation of the divine love, in the incarnation and suffering of the Son of God, is all that can give us peace and triumph in the last and utmost trial. Take the cross from Christianity and it is as if the sun were taken from the day and the stars from the night. Without the cross we have no Father in heaven to draw us to himself with the relentings and compassions of a father's heart; no inheritance of everlasting life made sure for our possession when the frail bark of our suffering mortality is wrecked upon the shores of time; no mansion of rest, offering repose to the weary soul, when the toil and the conflict of this earthly life are done. Without the cross there is no Friend of sinners on earth and no Lamb in the midst of the throne of heaven; no welcome for the wanderer who would return to the path of duty while he lives, no grace for the guilty in the final judgment. Without the cross, the powers of darkness are unconquerable, the punishment of sin is inevitable, there is nothing before us but a fearful looking for of judgment and fiery indignation which shall devour and destroy.

The cross alone can give us hope and victory in the last and utmost trial. The subtleties of philosophy, the refinements of taste, the difficulties of scepticism, the seductions of pleasure, the indifference of worldliness are idle mockeries to the man who has looked upon this world for the last time, and who is just about to know, by experience, the awful secret of death and eternity. Even then, the way before him shall be full of light, and he shall advance with the step of a conqueror, if he can see the cross of Christ uplifted on the distant heights and shining through the gloom.

On a summer's day, in the hottest month of the year, I was climbing the mountain wall which separates the Canton Vallais from Uri in Switzerland. There was no house, no human form, no voice of man or beast to relieve the awful desolation around me. Nothing broke the deep silence, save the roar of the torrents in the distance below, and the occasional rush of sliding snows from the heights above. The pine groves and the green pastures, where shepherds kept their flocks, were far beneath. In every direction the blue dome of the sky rested upon icy peaks and walls of gleaming snow. In every direction the prospect closed with scenes of the most sublime and horrible desolation.

Weary, panting for breath in the thin air, heated with toil, and yet chilled with blasts that swept from the winter's eternal throne, I paused many times to rest from exhaustion, many times looked back longingly towards the green valley, where the "arrowy Rhone" rushed forth a strong river from beneath the melting glacier; many times I gazed upward to the cold height, which seemed to lift itself away into the clouds as fast as I labored up the steep, while every fibre of my weary frame protested that I could climb no higher. Many times I thought how fearful a thing it would be to die there alone; many times feared that it had been an act of rashness to attempt the ascent without a guide or a friend, till at last I saw before me, and but a few steps further on, a CROSS, a high firm broad cross, standing amid desolate rocks and wintry snows; and I knew that when I reached that cross, there would be no other height to climb, and beyond was a descending and easy path, to beautiful vales and laughing streams and the cheerful homes of men.

At the sight of that cross, standing amid clouds and snow to mark the utmost height of the pass, I felt something of the enthusiasm with which the Romish devotee clasps and kisses the symbol of the world's redemption.

And as I passed leisurely and joyously on, in my subsequent journey, I thought many times to myself,—oh! how hard it is to climb the cold and weary mountains of separation which sin and unbelief have raised up between us and the blessed cross of Christ. How determined and persevering the exertion that we must put forth, if we would ever reach it. And when we look back, how inviting the beautiful vales of ease and self-indulgence appear in the distance. But once reach the cross and the great joy begins, the great conflict ends. At the foot of the cross, the penitent and believing soul has reached the highest elevation, above all the foes of his peace, and he thence looks forth a king and a conqueror, upon a subject world. The devotees of earthly pleasure have no joy, the sons of fame no triumph, to be compared with that which fills the weary and burdened sinner's heart, when he looks for the first time in faith upon the cross of Christ.

THE END.

www.ingramcontent.com/pod-product-compliance
Lightning Source LLC
Chambersburg PA
CBHW020237240426

43672CB00006B/556